Wounded Soul Rejoice

Evelyn Walters

Wounded Soul

Notice

Wounded Soul Rejoice
Copyright © 2019 by Evelyn Walters

All rights reserved. No part of this book may be reproduced or transmitted in any form or by any means without the written permission of the author.

ISBN 978-1-9990591-0-1

The majority of quotes used in this book come from the New King James Version (NKJV) Bible. The King James Version (KJV) Bible and Amplified (AMP) Bible are also used and noted as such.

Contact us:

EvelynWalters@live.com

Edited by:

**StellarWork Editing
Natasha@stellarwork.info**

Cover design and page layout:

**Jerry Mensah (J Mens Dreams Studios)
Jmens027@yahoo.com**

Table of Contents

Dedication	7
Introduction	9
My Story – A brief Background	13
Younger Years Stolen	17
My Later Teen Years	23
My Education	27
Getting Understanding in God and His Word	35
The Healing Process – Letting Go	39
After The Rain	43
Let the Peace of God Rule in your Heart	55
The Light of the World	59
The Story Behind Wounded Soul Rejoice	61
Beside Quiet Waters	65
Moving Forward	71
Find your Place in God	83
Rejoice in the Lord Always	87
Pray, Believe and Without Fail, Recover All	93
See Love through the Eyes of Christ	105
The Beauty of Holiness	121
The Life Changing Power of God	125
True Success	131
Conclusion	145
Poem: You Will Soon Recover	149
About the Author	151

AKNOWLEDGEMENT

I would like to thank my sister Marcia, whom I believe God placed in my life strategically as a support system during my healing process.

DEDICATION

This book is dedicated to all the precious souls that have been through hardships in their lives. My prayer is that you will find healing, deliverance, and the power of forgiveness. Realize that God has blessed you with this life for you to enjoy and not for you to live in fear. My hope is for you to be free in Jesus' name, and most of all, that you will be showered with God's amazing, undying love.

"For God so loved the world that He gave His only begotten son that whosoever believes in Him should not perish but shall have everlasting life" (John 3:16).

INTRODUCTION
God Will Heal Your Wounds

"He heals the brokenhearted and binds up their wounds" (Psalms 147:3).

There are often situations in our lives that make us wonder if anyone cares; but Jesus cares! At times you may feel like no one understands what you're going through, however the Lord does, and He wants you to know that He loves you, regardless of your circumstances. "Greater love has no one than this, than to lay down one's life for his friends" (John 15:13).

As believers in Christ, we are friends of the Lord. Jesus wants us to share our deepest thoughts, hopes and desires with Him, even though He already knows what they are. Before we were formed in our mother's womb, He knew us: "Before I formed thee in the belly I knew thee; and before thou camest forth out of the womb I sanctified thee, and I ordained thee a prophet unto the nations" (Jeremiah 1:5 KJV).

It is good for us to communicate with the Lord on a daily basis, and to remember that our Heavenly Father knows what is best for us. And when one has been wounded, healing is necessary. Picture this: a wound left unattended for a period of time will get infected, and no matter what part of your body it is in, that wound will definitely affect the rest of your body. For as we know that each member of our body is fitly joined together by God, one limb cannot do without the other. "But now God has set the members, each one of them, in the body just as He pleased" (1 Corinthians 12:18).

Once infection sets in, your body will not be able to function accordingly. That is why we seek a physician early, to prevent the infection from spreading to the whole body.

The same is true with a spiritual wound, which affects the whole spirit. Let's say you've been wounded by someone who allowed themselves to be used by the enemy, and as a result, they left you physically, mentally and emotionally wounded. These are some very deep spiritual wounds that you cannot always see on the outside. This is one reason why we should never judge the actions of people around us, for we never know what that individual has been through. Yet although these wounds cannot be seen, they require immediate attention! And the attention needed comes from the one who heals the broken heart and binds our wounds (Psalms 147:3).

"For I will restore health unto thee, and I will heal thee of thy wounds, saith the Lord: because they called thee an Outcast, saying, This is Zion, whom no man seeketh after" (Jeremiah 30:17 KJV).

There is no use in seeking revenge towards those who have done you harm: "For we know him that hath said, Vengeance belongeth unto me, I will recompense, saith the Lord. And again, The Lord shall judge his people" (Hebrews 10:30 KJV). Instead, allow the Lord to shower you with His love. God hears your cry and He will rush to your rescue.

"I love the Lord, because He has heard my voice and my supplications" (Psalms 116:1). Just put your trust in the Almighty God. Jesus never fails! He is El Shaddai – the Almighty, All-Sufficient God. He has the power to make all things possible, notably your healing and restoration. "But He said, 'The things which are impossible with men are possible with God'" (Luke 18:27).

> Bless the Lord, O my soul;
> And all that is within me, bless His holy name!
> Bless the Lord, O my soul,
> And forget not all His benefits:
> Who forgives all your iniquities,
> Who heals all your diseases…
> (Psalms 103:1-3)

CHAPTER 1
My Story – A brief Background

My life began on May 20, 1973 (according to man's time; God's time is different). I was born in Kingston, Jamaica. There is not much I remember about my life there, but I can recall leaving the island at the age of three. You must be thinking how one could remember at such a young age. You would be surprised to know what children remember; in our memory banks are events that occurred in our lives – some good and perhaps some traumatizing. You would be surprised to know what I remember. I believe that the Lord has blessed me with a tremendous memory.

I can recall getting on the airplane and immediately, I started to cry. I really wanted to go back home. We flew over the vast body of water known as the Caribbean Ocean. The few words I spoke to my mother were: "The plane is going to fall into the ocean!" She laughed at me and said, "That won't happen." I was so afraid; all I could do was cry. Maybe it wasn't the best idea for my mother to put me in the window seat, where I could see just about everything from the window. The flight attendant gave me toys and candy to calm me down, and tried everything to convince me that nothing bad was going to happen.

Starting our new life in Canada was a great change for us all and it was still summertime when we arrived. My mother and older brother were really excited and looking forward to our new life in Ottawa.

Our plane first landed in the city of Toronto. My brother was amazed by all the pretty lights as he glanced out of the window. He was four and a half years old. I was not really interested in looking out the window, recalling how traumatized I was doing so while we were still in the air. Once we landed at the airport, I was so happy the ride was over. We were then greeted by happy relatives who showed us a lot of love.

As soon as winter began, the cold and the snow came as a shock to us coming from a tropical island. When I first looked at the snow, I didn't know what it was or what would happen if I stepped on it. It was the first time I ever felt the cool winter breeze and saw snow everywhere; talk about a wakeup call. Immediately I started crying for fear of the cold. One could assume that I would have been excited about the snow. Well, that wasn't the case for me. My father once told me I was so tiny at three years old that while I was walking with my grandmother outside, suddenly I fell in the snow and no one could find me!

The snow wasn't all that bad; it was white and glittery – such an awesome sight. On the warm winter days, when the snow was freshly falling, my brother and I would go outside to play, building snowmen and snow forts. We always had so much fun together. There was nothing that could separate us.

I remember my mom buying me a new red snow suit, pink hat and matching scarf; they were my favorite and I was very happy! Nonetheless, I still didn't like the cold weather. My older brother loved the snow and would play in it all day long. I, on the other hand, would start crying as soon as I got cold, and that's when my grandmother would call me inside.

Growing up with my brother was the greatest. Till this day, we have a special bond that could never be broken.

Our first Christmas in Canada took place when I was four years old and my brother was five. Life was great and we had everything we needed. I remember receiving my first Tonka truck. They were as popular back then as they are today; every child had to have one. I also remember receiving a little doll with silky, long blonde hair and a lovely white dress. My brother received lots of Tonka trucks and cars. We were both thrilled. For us, life couldn't get any better. At this time my mother worked very hard to provide our daily necessities; she was an incredibly hard worker. She worked long, hard hours just to make sure we had everything we needed. My mother is a true blessing to my soul. I love her with all my heart.

Sometimes my brother and I could not understand why mom had to work so hard. At this time in our lives, we started spending more time with our grandmother and other close relatives who became our childcare providers.

I remember waking up one morning, only to catch a glimpse of my beloved mother as she was leaving to go to work. My brother and I were usually up early in the morning just to say goodbye to her. We would run to our mother's bedroom window and watch her walk to the bus stop, which was not too far away. On this particular day, there was freezing rain outside and my mother was expecting my younger brother at the time. The street was very slippery, and as my mother walked on the ice, she suddenly slipped and fell. My brother started laughing hysterically. I told him it wasn't funny as she could have hurt herself and the baby. My brother told me to be quiet, and I thought to myself, "How rude of him to say that." So when my mother got home, I made sure to tell her how my brother laughed at her, and to my surprise, she laughed also.

CHAPTER 2
Younger Years Stolen

"The thief does not come except to steal, and to kill, and to destroy. I have come that they may have life, and that they may have it more abundantly" (John 10:10).

I was five years old when the pain began. Most people I know enjoyed their childhood. As for me, most of my memories are filled with fear, pain, grief, darkness, sadness, betrayal and anger. These are the emotions that plagued my life as a young girl. You might ask what I could have possibly gone through at such a tender age to cause me to feel this way. Let me share a little with you.

You can imagine what the life of a normal little girl should be like. From my point of view, it should be a happy and fun time with family and friends. However, what I experienced as a young girl growing up was very different. I pray that no other young girl would have to go through such a trial – the terror of being sexually abused.

It was very hard for me to get by, thinking about the people who had been placed in my life to nurture and take care of me, but who resorted to such evil actions.

I had to endure the unimaginable at the hands of two of my uncles. I was often left in their care, only to be taken out of my bed in the middle of the night and brought to their beds to be used as a sexual toy. This is nobody's idea of a happy childhood.

I can't even begin to describe how traumatizing it was to have to endure this as a young girl. My intention is to help someone who may have experienced similar trauma. If this is you, know that you are not alone, and that there's hope for your healing and restoration.

Even at the age of five years old, I felt that what was happening to me was not right. This abuse went on for years, right up to when I turned 11 years old. I remember after each painful experience, my uncles would always promise to buy me nice things – like my first pair of skates and my first bicycle – if I didn't tell anyone about what they were doing to me. In most cases a child would be overjoyed to have these things. This made me believe that in order to get gifts, I first had to be abused. What a sad reality. Each time I was molested by my uncles, I became more and more fearful of people. The depressing thoughts I had only grew stronger along with the hatred and the resentment. My world was filled with sorrow and grief.

I remember I had a lot of friends while growing up, and the majority of them were girls. When I would hear about the fun things they did with their families, it gave me some joy because at least I could hear about good things happening to others where family was concerned. However, when I went home, I would just go into my bedroom and weep. Then I would ask myself why I couldn't be happy like my friends and have good things to talk about. I felt depressed, tormented and sad. What I didn't know at the time was that I was also grieving the loss of my innocence as a little girl.

I was also overwhelmed with the fear of having to sleep by myself. It was very hard for me so I would hold my pillows and squeeze my teddy bears, which brought some comfort. I felt safe at those moments, but I could not control my emotions during this time of my life. My emotions controlled me. Whenever I felt hurt – if other children made fun of me or if I failed at something – I would cry. I would cry for every little thing. Even if I lost something that belonged to me, I would start crying before I even attempted to look for it.

Every time one of my older family members had to go somewhere, they would leave me with my uncles. I would immediately begin to feel sad as I knew what usually happened when I was left alone with them. I used to wonder as a child how they felt about what they were doing to me, and how they could possibly think it was alright using me as they did. I was so confused, and I never really felt that I could tell anybody what I was going through. I thought that I would be sent away, and that no one would believe me. I battled with this nightmare for many years. I had so much fear that I couldn't even tell my mother, the one I felt closest to. It was too hard for me. I didn't want her to be angry at me; I didn't want her to hate me or her own brothers, because they looked up to her as the eldest of all their siblings.

I loved and still love my mother with all my heart, but I did not appreciate what I was going through. I felt that it was her responsibility to protect me from bad people and situations. I even started to have hatred and resentment towards my mother – that wonderful woman who gave birth to me, that God had blessed me with.

In my teenage years, my mother would share stories about how much trouble I would give her at times as a child. Some of them were actually funny, but as a teenager I realized that the things I did as a child were just my way of letting her know what I was feeling at the time. I yearned for her attention and love even more during these times, but wondered if she would ever take notice of me and question why I was such a mischievous child. So I attempted to stay closer to the family members that I knew would not hurt me: my siblings and cousins. And as time went by my younger siblings came along – four of them to be exact.

With each new addition to our family, my life began to have purpose. Joy and excitement began to overtake me when my brothers and sister were born. My mother let me assist in taking care of them – grooming them, feeding them, bathing them and simply enjoying playtime together. This is when my life began to take a different turn. My mother even allowed me to take my siblings for walks in the park. I held them and did all the fun things people do with their brothers and sisters.

Happiness was rising up in my heart and I felt like my life was finally getting better. Now I was the big sister that everyone looked up to. I felt I had the greatest life because I was a big sister and I had the company of my siblings to take away my feelings of being afraid and alone. So you can see how easy it became for me to suppress all of my painful childhood memories. Yet, looking back at this moment, I wholeheartedly believe that God sent my siblings into my life to change me and to change the way I was feeling about life. This became part of my healing process.

CHAPTER 3
My Later Teen Years

Some may ask how I could even remember these things that happened to me. At the age of 16, the painful memories I had suppressed began to resurface. They started replaying in my mind like a movie. By this time, my younger siblings were also getting older and taking care of them became less joyful and more overwhelming – especially considering what I was beginning to go through myself. My mother had great expectations of me, and they were amplified as she went through a separation with her husband. This brought great pressure on me because my responsibilities increased. It became too much for me to handle, having to take care of my siblings as well as being the listening ear of support for my mother during her separation.

I simply had too much on my plate. While I was sympathetic to what my mother was going through, my feelings and emotions began getting the best of me. I was trying so hard to forget my own painful memories that I just wanted to avoid every possible negative situation.

Growing up feeling as if I could never share or tell anyone what I was feeling was not easy for me. I had bottled up all of these harmful feelings inside of me for years. I truly felt like a bomb waiting to explode. I felt trapped, like a prisoner inside my own body. I wanted to be freed from that prison but felt there was no one to help me. I always wondered how I could ever get passed these overwhelming feelings and emotions.

I was confused and did not trust any male. I made sure that I stayed away from them. One thing I thought would help me get away from my feelings was to visit my good friend after school every once in a while. After school visits soon turned into weekends, and then weekends turned into weeks, until I finally decided to run away from home at the age of 17.

I felt that if I ran away from my problems and responsibilities, all of my painful memories would go away. However, this did not turn out to be true; it only made things worse. And my life began to spin into a whirlwind of rebellion. The hatred I felt towards my mother grew, to the point that I was telling others how much I despised her for what had happened to me in my childhood. So when I decided to run away for good, I believed I had made the best decision of my life. I felt freedom in that moment as I had no responsibilities to hold me down. Well, that was what I thought back then.

At that time in my life, I began not to care about how my mother felt or what kind of stress I was causing her. It was almost as if I wanted her to experience the loss of something because then maybe she would know what I had been going through.

I had only succeeded once again in suppressing the memories of my childhood abuse. It seemed like I was in a safe place in my life, but what a deception. I was hanging out with the wrong crowd, partying, drinking, smoking, shoplifting, and being promiscuous. I often found myself in situations I didn't want to be in.

I was raped on two occasions, but was afraid of taking any of those men to court as I feared for my life. So I just hid away. I even began to feel that I deserved what happened to me.

I remember going to the hospital after being assaulted and having to go through the procedure of accumulating evidence through means of what the police call a rape kit. Every moment felt so degrading. I felt as if I was living my childhood all over again, and crawling back into that shell of isolation. Some of my friends at that time tried to find out what was troubling me because they knew that I was usually a fun-loving person. To see me in such an emotionally wrecked state concerned them. I never completely shared with them what I was going through. I would always just resort to telling them how dysfunctional my relationship with my mother was. Then my friends would try to console me by telling me jokes or doing things that would make me laugh and I would forget about the painful memories. This only lasted for a moment. The memories of my past would resurface at times when I was alone or when I experienced disappointments. I felt like my life was always going through an emotional cycle of pain and defeat.

CHAPTER 4
My Education

"And He said to me, 'My grace is sufficient for you, for My strength is made perfect in weakness.' Therefore most gladly I will rather boast in my infirmities, that the power of Christ may rest upon me" (2 Corinthians 12:9).

Junior kindergarten right up to grade 11 was very difficult for me. I found it extremely hard to focus on my school work. I was also quite timid; looking back I see that I lacked self-confidence and had low self-esteem.

I remember always being afraid to truly express the way I was feeling and never liked to stand in front of the class and do presentations, for I feared rejection. When other students would laugh at me for making a mistake, it was the worst feeling ever.

I did try to work hard at every task I was given, and there were always students at every stage of my schooling that I considered to be 'the brain', as they made the hardest task look so easy. You could always find me staying close to them, asking questions and seeking their help. I often wondered how they were so smart and knew the answer to every question, standing in amazement at how brilliant they were, but never truly understanding the most basic principles of learning.

Math was always the subject I succeeded the least in. In the beginning it was not so bad; I did well with addition and subtraction. But when it came to multiplication, my mind could not fully grasp the concept. I often needed one-on-one help throughout my schooling, and at times I would be placed in what was referred to as special education. I am very thankful for the teachers I had at school as they looked out for me when they realized that I needed extra help and attention.

A few of my favorite hobbies growing up were reading and writing poetry and short stories. During my early teen years, I also enjoyed reading romance novels. I embraced the thought of love and romance, and it encouraged me to read about the hardships the couples would go through, which most of the time would lead to a happy ending. It gave me hope to see that no matter what people go through in life, no matter the storms they may face, the sun eventually shines again.

Grade 8 was a wonderful year for me. My English teacher noticed that I wrote poetry and short stories very well. He was really impressed and would continually encourage me to keep up the great work. This gave me confidence.

I started feeling better about myself, and I finally was able to accept compliments. I started doing better in all other subjects – even math. Although math never became one of my strongest subjects, I was able to make it through and I am thankful that I did. I learned a lot about myself and about family during these years, and I started to ponder more and more about what I wanted out of life.

Grade 9, however, was bothersome to me. I began to feel worthless and without purpose. Most of my friends were talking about what they wanted to do after high school, what field they wanted to study in, and here I was twiddling my thumbs because I never really took the time to sit and think about what I wanted to do with my life. The responsibility of taking care of siblings weighed heavily upon me.

I did enjoy playing with hair and makeup as long as I could remember, so I took a cosmetology and barbering course in grade 9, 10 and 11. My teacher told me that I was very good at hairdressing and this was one of the classes I enjoyed and took pride in. My marks were high in this class and on a few occasions, the teacher pulled me aside to ask me about my career aspirations. He told me he had noticed that I had good hands when it came to dealing with every aspect of hairdressing, and asked if I would ever consider going to college to take a hairdressing course. I said I would consider it but I would have to discuss it with my mother first. So I did that, but sadly my mother didn't show much interest in what I wanted to do. This was a sad time for me because my mother gave more attention to my younger siblings and their needs, which to me meant that she favored them over me. This troubled and discouraged me at the same time. As I look back at these times I wonder how a parent could favor one child over another. I never could understand this because each one of us is the apple of God's eye, and He loves us all the same.

I found the year I spent in grade 10 to be depressing, and I started losing interest in school, skipping classes and just being rebellious.

I eventually dropped out of high school all together in the early part of grade 11. I was in a relationship at that time and became pregnant. I tried to attend classes for three months but it became very hard for me, so I decided stay home throughout the rest of my pregnancy with the hopes of returning back to school after having the baby. Unfortunately that didn't happen. Two years later, I became pregnant with my second son and decided to be a stay-at-home mom.

By the time my youngest son was eight months old, I started contemplating going back to school. I ended up putting both my children in daycare so that I could achieve my goals. The Lord provided and I got accepted for a subsidy, which meant that my childcare fees would be paid for by the government as long as I was enrolled in a program that would make my family life better. At this time I was on welfare and other government benefits so I did not have to work, which would have been too much with everything I had on my plate as a single mother of two going back to school.

Going back to school was a huge challenge for me but I was determined to improve my family's quality of life. So I went to a business college and enrolled as a mature student without my grade 12 diploma. I took a business and accounting program and stuck it out for six months of intensive work. This involved lots of studying, exams and assignments, which was overwhelming at times with the added responsibility of raising two young children and having to wake up at 6:00 a.m. Monday to Friday in order to get them to daycare for 7:00 a.m., then having to go back home and get ready for class at 9:00 a.m.

I don't know what I was thinking choosing the program I did, having to take accounting and bookkeeping while I never enjoyed math. I was not very excited about it but I gave it my best, got extra help from a classmate, and I attained the passing mark, although feeling that I could have done better. For some reason my brain would just block out anything that had to do with mathematics. Nonetheless, I successfully completed my course and received my certificate.

At first I was thinking about working in a bank but that was not where my heart was. So I began to apply for administrative jobs since I decided that accounting wasn't for me.

After months of consistent job searching, handing out and faxing resumes, I gave up because my hard work wasn't paying off, and at the few interviews I went to, I was asked to provide a high school diploma, which became a roadblock for me.

Nonetheless, instead of getting discouraged I decided to complete my high school education. I chose to take my courses by correspondence so that I could take care of my two young children at the same time; and this is how I finally obtained my high school diploma. I made a schedule for myself and whenever my children were at home, I would wait until they had their afternoon nap and hit the books. Every day at the same time I would study and complete my assignments. I managed to hand them in on time and attained high marks.

One day while sitting at my kitchen table, I asked the Lord why I didn't get these marks in high school. And the Lord said to me that my head was in the clouds, that I had too many distractions at that time.

This taught me that it's never too late to accomplish a goal, and that the key is to stay focused and determined to accomplish the task at hand.

Through the challenging times, prayer became an important part of my life. I mean, I prayed about everything, always seeking God's direction. What sense would it make to go after something not knowing whether it is God's will for my life? I felt that I wasted so much time in the business and accounting program that I didn't want to go blindly into anything like that again.

Yet the Lord brought me through college again. Before I even considered going back to school, however, the Lord had to reveal to me that this was part of His perfect plan for my life.

One day I was at a career information session unrelated to the medical field, and the Lord used three people that same day to ask me the same question. This was a bit strange to me, and we know the Lord works in mysterious ways. By the time the third person approached me, I was already convinced that the Lord was confirming that going to college was what He wanted me to do. The question that all three asked me was if I had experience in the medical field. This almost blew my mind, as I was thinking of taking a medical office administration course, and their question was the answer I was waiting for.

My best friend, Sharon is the one that the Lord used to help me take the first step by helping me find the resources and government grant to aid in the application for the medical course, and by God's grace, I successfully completed the course.

As a single mother with two children, getting through school and college was challenging; however, God came through for us, continuously making a way where there seemed to be no way.

The devil tried to get me depressed and discouraged, but God is my counsellor, my healer and my deliverer – Jesus is my all. I have learned that I can only experience success in the Lord, for there is no failure in Him. Jesus won the victory for us once and for all, and for every situation we may face in life. *Thank you, Lord!*

CHAPTER 5
Getting Understanding in God and His Word

> "How much better to get wisdom than gold! And to get understanding is to be chosen rather than silver" (Proverbs 16:16).

My life only started to make sense once I surrendered all to the Lord.

Sometimes it's hard to explain things; but when you know God for yourself, He gives you understanding in all things. Knowing His Word plays a huge part in our lives. The Word of the Lord teaches us everything we need to know in order to be effective and a true witness in this present life. What always grabs ahold of me is the fact that the Bible shows us who we are. Even when we fall or fail, we have the opportunity and privilege to come to God in prayer, using His Word, for example: "Create in me a clean heart, O God; and renew a right spirit within me. Cast me not away from thy presence; and take not thy holy spirit from me. Restore unto me the joy of thy salvation; and uphold me with thy free spirit" (Psalms 51:10-12 KJV).

The Word of God is a manual for living a pure and victorious life in the Lord. While we are here on earth, there are so many principles to learn from God's Word that there isn't enough ink or paper on which to write it all down!

Following His instructions, whether from His Word or by the leading of His Holy Spirit, is vital – especially when dealing with healing.

As the Lord leads you through your healing process, take note of His instructions on how to stay healed and free in Jesus Christ.

One day, I was attending an appointment that had to do with my healing. As I stepped outside I was going straight, and then I sensed the Lord telling me to turn right; so in obedience I followed the instruction. As I was walking, I felt a lovely cool breeze. It was a beautiful, sunny day.

I then proceeded to walk over a bridge, and I heard the voice of the Lord say to me, "Evelyn, just as you are walking over this bridge – not looking back at your past – continue moving forward into your future, for it is bright."

When I get a word from the Lord, I never forget it. I remember it as it was yesterday, and I thank the Lord for this particular one which changed my life. It is now my endeavor to encourage those going through challenges of their own with those same words, to urge them not to fall back into the mess the Lord has delivered, healed and saved them from, but to move forward, leaving all those trials behind.

> "Brethren, I do not count myself to have apprehended; but one thing I do, forgetting those things which are behind and reaching forward to those things which are ahead, I press toward the goal for the prize of the upward call of God in Christ Jesus" (Philippians 3:13-14).

CHAPTER 6
The Healing Process – Letting Go

"…casting all your cares [all your anxieties, all your worries, and all your concerns, once and for all] on Him, for He cares about you [with deepest affection, and watches over you very carefully]" (1 Peter 5:7 AMP).

I remember a time back in 2004 when I was going through a training session for a new job with the government. I had an ingrown finger nail and I decided to pull it out myself, which was a big mistake. It was so painful that it seemed to hit a nerve. A few days went by and I noticed my finger was swollen and red.

Then a day later, there was a yellow dot on the nail; this is when the infection was beginning to set in. Even though it was something so small and simple, this infection started to affect me and it was all I was thinking about.

When I showed it to my supervisor, she said that I needed to go to the hospital so I took her advice. When I got to the hospital, the doctor told me it was infected to the point that a minor surgery had to be performed. The doctor had to first freeze my finger, which was no fun because I don't like needles. This was the middle finger on my right hand, and I remember the excruciating pain I experienced. I looked away as the doctor injected the needle into my finger but it was still painful. My finger was now frozen as the doctor explained every step of what he was about to do, and I felt uneasy. First, he slit my finger so that the infection could run out. Then he cleaned the area and I felt relief. Right after that, he told me that I needed a vaccination shot, which meant another needle. (You can imagine the expression on my face.)

This vaccination was given in my upper arm and boy did I feel it. The doctor told me it would have been better to have received it in my right forearm because it was already hurting from the procedure to my finger. Clearly at this point it was too late.

After the surgery, the doctor gave me the strict instruction to never pull out an ingrown nail again.

This story is to show how the things we leave unattended, no matter how small they may seem to us at first, can and will cause problems for us. This is also true for spiritual matters and demonstrates the importance of taking all of our burdens and giving them over to the Lord, for indeed He cares for us (1 Peter 5:7). And when one part of the body is injured it needs to be healed because it will affect the other parts as well, if neglected.

The following scripture, which uses examples of our physical body parts to represent the body of Christ, or the Church, could also very well be applied to taking care our spiritual well-being and the importance of not leaving any emotional wound unattended:

> And those *members* of the body which we think to be less honorable, on these we bestow greater honor; and our unpresentable *parts* have greater modesty, but our presentable *parts* have no need. But God composed the body, having given greater honor to that *part* which lacks it, that there should be no schism in the body, but *that* the members should have the same care for one another. And if one member suffers, all the members suffer with *it;* or if one member is honored, all the members rejoice with *it.*
> (1 Corinthians 12:23- 26)

> "If the whole body were an eye, where would be the hearing? If the whole were hearing, where would be the smelling? But now God has set the members, each one of them, in the body just as He pleased. And if they were all one member, where would the body be?"
> (1 Corinthians 12:17-18)

CHAPTER 7
After The Rain

I can tell you that after the rain, you will smile again. It is after the rain that new life begins. Storm clouds will roll away and you will never be the same. Why should we worry, why should we fret when Jesus is our provider, and all of our needs are already met?

When God makes you a promise, you can trust Him at His Word. He will come through for you. In the book of Genesis, the Lord promises Sarah that she would have a son in her old age: "And the Lord visited Sarah as He had said, and the Lord did for Sarah as He had spoken. For Sarah conceived and bore Abraham a son in his old age, at the set time of which God had spoken to him" (Genesis 21:1-3).

The Lord is unique in all His ways; He will visit you at any time and at any place in your life, even when you least expect it. The Lord made a promise to Abraham, and Sarah laughed and did not believe: "Now Abraham and Sarah were old, well advanced in age; *and* Sarah had passed the age of childbearing. Therefore Sarah laughed within herself, saying, 'After I have grown old, shall I have pleasure, my lord being old also?'" (Genesis 18:11-12)

What God said to Abraham next is amazing: "Why did Sarah laugh, saying, 'Shall I surely bear *a child,* since I am old?' Is anything too hard for the Lord? At the appointed time I will return to you, according to the time of life, and Sarah shall have a son" (Genesis 18:13).

We can clearly see that Sarah did not believe what the Lord had promised to her and her husband, Abraham. When God makes you a promise, He will surely keep it and bring it to pass in His time.

While I was going through a rough season, the Lord spoke these words to me: "The time of your deliverance is now." At that point in my life I was not sure what He was speaking about, so I just took God at His Word. The Lord will speak to your heart on issues and pains of your past that need to be rooted out of your spirit.

There was a time when I didn't know what to do in order to receive healing and deliverance from the abuse I suffered in childhood. Many years of my life went by, and as I grew in the wisdom and knowledge of the Lord, my relationship with Jesus Christ grew stronger. Little did I know that my life was on its way to changing for the better, for God's glory, and that He had a wonderful plan for me. As I began to spend more time in prayer, it helped me to understand that what I had been through was to help others who are struggling from similar situations, and to get to a higher place in God. My relationship with the Lord continues to grow stronger each day. I can say that prayer is very important in every believer's life, for this is how we get closer to God – by spending quality time with Him.

At the time when trials and storms started to confront me and the support from those which I depended on all these years was not there, I felt extremely alone and rejected.

Remember this when you are going through hard times and you feel that no one is there: Jesus is standing right there with you. When you realize this, life doesn't feel lonely anymore.

This is the way Jesus felt in the garden of Gethsemane, when He asked His disciples to wait up for Him:

> Then Jesus came with them to a place called Gethsemane, and said to the disciples, "Sit here while I go and pray over there" And He took with Him Peter and the two sons of Zebedee, and He began to be sorrowful and deeply distressed. Then He said to them, "My soul is exceedingly sorrowful, even to death. Stay here and watch with Me." He went a little farther and fell on His face, and prayed, saying, "O My Father, if it is possible, let this cup pass from Me; nevertheless, not as I will, but as You *will.*" Then He came to the disciples and found them sleeping, and said to Peter,

"What! Could you not watch with Me one hour? Watch and pray, lest you enter into temptation. The spirit indeed *is* willing, but the flesh *is* weak."
(Matthew 26:36-41)

When you are going through the storms of your life, get closer to God. When you are in what seems to be the valley, or lowest point of your life, draw nearer to the Lord, and He will reveal His love, grace and mercy to you more and more. To record all that the Lord has done for us is almost impossible, for again, there is not enough ink or paper in this world to take note of it all. The goodness of God in our lives is never ending.

This book and what the Lord has inspired me to share with you is just the tip of the iceberg, and for all that the Lord has caused me to become, all the glory and praise belongs to Him. We are gifted to bless others so I'm offering my gifts back to God by sharing them with others.

How awesome is our God that He knows just what to say and do at precisely the right time. Knowing this, in all things we must wait on the Lord. In Psalms 62:1-2, David writes: "Truly my soul silently waits for God; From Him comes my salvation. He only is my rock and my salvation; He is my defense; I shall not be greatly moved." In Psalms 62:5-8, he writes, "My soul, wait silently for God alone, For my expectation is from Him. He only is my rock and my salvation; He is my defense; I shall not be moved. In God is my salvation and my glory; The rock of my strength, and my refuge, is in God. Trust in Him at all times, you people; Pour out your heart before Him; God is a refuge for us. Selah."

After the flood, God made a covenant with Noah and every living thing upon the earth that He would never destroy the earth with a flood again. "Thus I establish My covenant with you: Never again shall all flesh be cut off by the waters of the flood; never again shall there be a flood to destroy the earth" (Genesis 9:11).

The Lord keeps His promises, as it is written in the scripture below.

> And God said: "This *is* the sign of the covenant which I make between Me and you, and every living creature that *is* with you, for perpetual generations: I set My rainbow in the cloud, and it shall be for the sign of the covenant between Me and the earth. It shall be, when I bring a cloud over the earth, that the rainbow shall be seen in the cloud; and I will remember My covenant which *is* between Me and you and every living creature of all flesh; the waters shall never again become a flood to destroy all flesh. The rainbow shall be in the cloud, and I will look on it to remember the everlasting covenant between God and every living creature

of all flesh that *is* on the earth." And God said to Noah, "This *is* the sign of the covenant which I have established between Me and all flesh that *is* on the earth."
(Genesis 9:12-17)

I say that it is time to inherit the promise, and not put our own limits on God as Sarah did in Genesis 21:1-8, when she laughed at God's promise. In this story we are encouraged not to put limits on God, for He is able to do all things.

When we put limits on what we think the Lord can do, it can slow down our healing process and can hold back God's blessings. Again, it is far better to cast all our cares upon the Lord, for He cares for us (1 Peter 5:7). God is the only one who can heal and deliver us from the shame of our past.

Just look at how the Lord caused the sun to shine once again in the life of Abraham and Sarah through their son, Isaac. I believe that God can and will do for us all that He did time and again for those in the Bible who trusted in Him with their whole hearts. It is no secret what God can do, and what He's done for others He will do for you as well. And with arms wide open, He will pardon you. He says it in His Word.

Thunderstorms are a good representation of the personal challenges we face every day. When it rains, it pours. Storm clouds rise and billows roll, but trust in the Lord, for He is the sunshine after the rain. The rainbow He used to remind us of His covenant with the earth can also be a token for us to remember His individual promises towards each and every one of us. When the lightening is flashing, God is on the battle field for us and His warrior angels are working to destroy the prince of the air.

Our personal victory truly depends on our relationship with the Lord, because by acquiring and sharpening the gift of spiritual discernment, we know when there is spiritual warfare going on in the atmosphere, and that our arms need to be up.

The Word says, "For every one that useth milk is unskilful in the word of righteousness: for he is a babe. But strong meat belongeth to them that are of full age, even those who by reason for use have their senses exercised to discern both good and evil" (Hebrews 5:14 KJV).

After the Rain Comes the Rainbow

I am fascinated with the rainbow. After a sun shower, there is always a rainbow, and no matter where I am, I will literally run to a window or outside just to see the beauty of it.

One day, I was at home just having a wonderful time in the presence of the Lord during my devotional time with Him. The Lord suddenly told me to look out the window. And there it was, the most beautiful rainbow I had ever seen, and it wasn't even raining that day. At that moment, I knew that the Lord had done this just for me. There was such joy in my spirit as a glared at it; the Lord just knew how to make my day. So I said, "Lord, I would love to see another rainbow." And this just kept the spring in my step for the day.

I had a few errands to do that day, and as I walked up the road, the Lord made me change my direction. He said, "Go this way," and as I turned the corner, I looked up and saw two rainbows in the sky! At that moment, the joyfulness I already had just increased as I said, "Lord, you are so faithful." The Lord filled my heart with gladness once again on that day.

That was the only time in my life that I had ever seen what people call a double rainbow. The memory of it still puts a smile on my face this very day. And I say, *"Thank you, Jesus!"*

Yes, after the rain there is much relief. The storm clouds fade away, the birds begin to sing again and the grass is greener. You see blue skies and white clouds; even nature begins to be thankful.

Again I say, *"Thank you, Lord,"* for the storms, the rain, and the comfort through my pain. A smile has formed on my face and through it all I have learned to trust in Jesus. After the rain, you *will* smile again.

God will pour out His blessings upon our lives and it's up to us to prepare the field of our hearts to receive them.

The Reality of Our Warfare

We cannot ignore that there is warfare going on, and it will not end until Jesus, the King of Kings, comes back. We must realize that our stubborn enemy, the devil, will not stop because it's his job to attack the true child of God who is living a Christ-like life.

As a Christian, something must be wrong if you are not experiencing any attack from the enemy. We can expect to have some kind of affliction in our lives which is caused by our adversary, the devil, for his warfare is against the righteous. "Many are the afflictions of the righteous, But the Lord delivers him out of them all" (Psalms 34:19).

For this reason, we need to be prayer warriors and fight the good fight, in Jesus' name. We all have a mission, and we are the vessels that God has chosen to win the lost souls into His kingdom. We have to become conscious of the spiritual warfare, and also know that Satan has very limited power compared to the power that has been given to us in Christ Jesus.

While we stand against the weapons of the enemy, we must put on the whole armor of God and be on guard at all times, never letting our shield down. This means holding on to our integrity and being ready to fight. It is important not to be careless in our stand for the Lord, to continue to walk in the paths of righteousness and take everything to the Lord in prayer. "Put on the whole armor of God, that you may be able to stand against the wiles of the devil" (Ephesians 6:11).

It is also vital to be spiritually aware of our surroundings and environment by staying in prayer, and devoting our time to hearing from God.

Lord, I pray that you open our spiritual eyes and ears that we will not become victims to the snares of the enemy, and give us the grace to follow in obedience, in Jesus' name. We need your divine wisdom in our lives to make it. Have your way, Lord Jesus.

Let's be aware of who our shepherd and master is, for the Lord has great power over our lives, and He is able to deliver anyone from the condemnation and the bondage of sin. He will continue to guide us and all we have to do is to put our trust in Him, and we do that by giving our entire lives to Jesus Christ.

In this life, we will encounter trouble, even as Christians, but it helps to remember that the divine presence of the Lord is with us, and to allow His spirit and supernatural power to govern our lives, for He is able to do all things. So let us be encouraged and confident in the Lord.

CHAPTER 8
Let the Peace of God Rule in your Heart

"And the peace of God, which passeth all understanding, shall keep your hearts and minds through Christ Jesus" (Philippians 4:7 KJV).

Life can bring disappointments, and at times we may feel that we have become a failure. We seem to forget that there is no failure in God, especially when we put our trust in Him. The devil's job is to try and destroy us and to deprive us of the joy of the Lord; but don't let anyone steal your joy. God is the only one who can give you perfect peace. Take God at His every word, for Jesus never fails, and He always keeps His promises.

Nothing compares to the peace of God. It is written, "Thou will keep him in perfect peace, whose mind is stayed on thee: because he trusteth in thee" (Isaiah 26:3 KJV). It is vital to trust in the Lord in all that we do so that we will reach our fullest potential in Him. The Lord will work everything out for us: "And we know that all things work together for good to them that love God, to them who are the called according to his purpose" (Romans 8:28).

Don't let the troubles of this life rob you of the peace that only God can give you; "And let the peace of God rule in your hearts, to the also ye are called in one body; and be ye thankful (Colossians 3:15 KJV). The Lord will never leave us comfortless: "Peace I leave with you, my peace I give unto you: not as the world giveth, give I unto you, let not your heart be troubled, neither let it be afraid" (John 14:27). Once the Lord has placed His peace in your heart, guard it with everything you have. Jesus will give you peace, even in the middle of the storm; just hold on to Him for He will never let you go.

We have been justified and now have peace with God: "Therefore being justified by faith, we have peace with God through our Lord Jesus Christ: by whom also we have access of the glory of God" (Romans 5:1-2).

The best thing we can do is learn from our mistakes, and use our experiences as stepping stones and help others. When you look back on your past, just give God thanks and ask Him to help you achieve success. The Lord will help you every step of the way.

When you trust the Lord, He has no other choice than to bless you, for that is what is written in His Word:

> For the Lord God is a sun and shield;
> The Lord will give grace and glory;
> No good thing will He withhold

From those who walk uprightly.
O Lord of hosts,
Blessed is the man who trusts in You!
(Psalms 84:11-12)

Finally it's very important to guard our minds in order for us to have peace as believers in Christ. We must be aware of the devil's devices and use them against him, for the Lord has given us power and it's His anointing that breaks every yolk of bondage. We live in a world that needs to be taught the Word of God. There are so many voices that bring confusion, and this is the plan of the enemy because he knows he can get into our minds and control us if he can get us to doubt the Word of God, or think thoughts that are destructive in nature. It's up to us to use the tools the Lord has given us to overcome every attack – most notably His Word.

It is of great importance to keep our minds on things that are good in nature:

Finally, brethren, whatever things are true, whatever things are noble, whatever things are just, whatever things are pure, whatever things are lovely, whatever things are of good report, if there is any virtue and if there is anything praiseworthy – meditate on these things."
(Philippians 4:8)

This is true because what we think about – what we let into our hearts – ends up determining the direction our lives take.

Therefore, think life; think about the things that bring life and peace to your spirit. Get God's Word into your mind and heart and you are guaranteed to walk in the perfect peace and victory that can only be found in The Lord.

"Keep your heart with all diligence,
For out of it spring the issues of life" (Proverbs 4:23).

CHAPTER 9
The Light of the World

"Then Jesus spoke to them again, saying, 'I am the light of the world. He who follows Me shall not walk in darkness, but have the light of life'" (John 8:12).

In order for us to enjoy an abundant life, we are to walk in the light of the Lord. When we have fellowship with the Lord, this light will illuminate in our hearts, and this is a special light that can be seen from the outside.

> It is right to give thanks and be joyful in the Lord. This is the message which we have heard of him, and declare unto you, that God is light, and in Him is no darkness at all. If we say that we have fellowship with Him, and walk in the light, as He is in the light, we have fellowship with one another.
> (1 John 1:5-7)

The love of the Lord is what causes us to shine for the Lord. Let your light shine, so those who are blinded by the darkness around them may acknowledge the light within us, which is Christ Jesus.

Proverbs 4:18 reads as follows: "But the path of the just is like the shining sun, that shines ever brighter unto the perfect day." Jesus has ordained us as right-living people to shine brightly and also to live a life of blessing, joy and peace, walking in the light and the peace of God. The Lord has called us to be a light of hope and a helping hand to others.

> By this we know love, because He laid down His life for us. And we also ought to lay down our lives for the brethren. But whoever has this world's goods, and sees his brother in need, and shuts up his heart from him, how does the love of God abide in him? My little children, let us not love in word or in tongue, but in deed and in truth.
> (1 John 3:16-17)

Let the love of God shower your heart and it will root out all the baggage and hate of the past that the devil would try to use to hinder you from going forward. We are all here to help one another. The Lord has not taken away His compassion towards us, so let us get to that place where we allow God to use our experiences and hurts to help other wounded souls.

CHAPTER 10
The Story Behind *Wounded Soul Rejoice*

"Rejoice in the Lord always. Again I will say, rejoice!"
(Philippians 4:4)

Just as the Lord encouraged me never to give up on my hopes and dreams, I want to encourage your wounded soul with this book. The Lord has really blessed me, and I now have a testimony to share with the world.

One evening while staying at a relative's home, as I slept I heard myself singing in the spirit, which was a very interesting experience. The words I heard in a beautiful melody were: "Wounded soul – never give up." These words began to repeat in my spirit, and I could hear myself signing them, but my lips weren't moving. It felt like I was in the clouds and the Lord was just lifting me up. Although it seemed like I was singing these words to myself, it was really the Lord dropping a song into my spirit. This was an awesome episode that I will never forget. Even though I was hearing my own voice singing, it sounded like a sweet melody from heaven.

The Lord then woke me up from my sleep and instructed me to write down these words: "Wounded soul – never give up!"

When the Lord drops something into your spirit – whether it is a song, a word, whatever it may be – pray and seek Him to find out exactly what He wants you to do with the information He has given you. He will direct you accordingly.

A few weeks later, after much prayer and fasting, the Lord revealed to me the topic of this book, along with a song that He inspired me to write. There are many wonderful things that I will be sharing when the time comes, God willing.

When you read *Wounded Soul Rejoice*, you might ask yourself what a wounded soul has to rejoice about. Well I can tell you with confidence that after the rain you *will* smile again; storm clouds shall pass away, new life shall begin, and you will never be the same.

The Lord makes all things beautiful in its time, and this is exactly what He has done with my life. I encourage you to wait on the Lord and follow His every instruction. He will take the pain of your wounded soul away. Jesus will take you through the hard times. You are not alone; put your trust in Him. He'll take you through it all and you will become a witness to others of His goodness:

> But rise and stand on your feet; for I have appeared to you for this purpose, to make you a minister and a witness both

of the things which you have seen and of the things which I will yet reveal to you. I will deliver you from the Jewish people, as well as from the Gentiles, to whom I now send you, to open their eyes, in order to turn them from darkness to light, and from the power of Satan to God, that they may receive forgiveness of sins and an inheritance among those who are sanctified by faith in Me.
(Acts 26:16-18)

Wherever you go, just shine and be who God has called you to be – the light of the world in Christ Jesus. When you are born again of God's Spirit, the light is so glorious, and when the fire of God is burning deep within your soul, it will propel you to reach out to others and win souls into His kingdom. Fire consumes, and when the devil tries to cool you down by blowing out your light, just ask the Lord to restore that fire and He will revive the Fire of the Holy Ghost within you.

Allow the Holy Spirit to speak peace to your heart and He will give you words that will speak to you. The Holy Spirit will comfort you with words of encouragement no matter what you're going through; He is your helper and comforter. Just listen to the message of love that springs forth, for it's the spirit of God that dwells within you reminding you that you are not alone and that He will be your guide.

When you hear from the Holy Spirit, He will let you know what to do, and as you follow in obedience, everything will be alright. Let the Holy Spirit bring comfort and hope to your heart today.

"Now the God of hope fill you with all joy and peace in believing, that ye may abound in hope, through the power of the Holy Ghost" (Romans 15:13).

CHAPTER 11
Beside Quiet Waters

After the storm, the Lord will lead you beside quiet waters, where you can find rest for your soul. And this perfect peace can only come from God – the kind of peace that will make you forget that you were ever wounded by the individuals who allowed themselves to be used by the devil to wound your soul.

When God brings you to this place of peace, and you begin to look forward, you are able to see the sun rising upon your life, bringing in a new day. Your tears have been washed away and your wounds have been healed by God, who is the great physician! Now you have the rest of your life to look forward to in the Lord. Psalm 23 illustrates this beautifully:

> The Lord is my shepherd;
> I shall not want.
> He makes me to lie down in green pastures;
> He leads me beside the still waters.
> He restores my soul;
> He leads me in the paths of righteousness
> For His name's sake.
> Yea, though I walk through the valley of the shadow of death,
> I will fear no evil;

For You are with me;
Your rod and Your staff, they comfort me.
You prepare a table before me in the presence of my enemies;
You anoint my head with oil;
My cup runs over.
Surely goodness and mercy shall follow me
All the days of my life;
And I will dwell in the house of the Lord
Forever.

To enjoy a place beside quiet waters, we need to get into the fullness of the Lord. We should never be at a place where we are comfortable, or complacent. One of the best ways to enjoy the fullness of God's presence is through prayer. In Acts 3:1, Peter and John decided to go to church together, and their sole purpose was to pray: "Now Peter and John went up together to the temple at the hour of prayer, the ninth hour" (Acts 3:1). This is one of the many ways we can get closer to the Lord – by talking and conversing with Him. He is just a prayer away.

The things that we need for our Christian journey are in the Word of the Lord, and in His presence, and we enter His presence with a grateful heart and with words (or songs) of praise: "Enter into His gates with thanksgiving, And into His courts with praise. Be thankful to Him, and bless His name" (Psalms 100:4).

And when you enter His presence, expect to receive a blessing from the Lord. Request a word from the Lord; just one word will remove any doubt and cause the sun to shine by giving you peace of mind. *Speak to us, Lord.*

Don't just stand at the gate; enter into the presence of God, into the inner court, the Holy of Holies – the place of worship.

It's all about Jesus; everything we do as Christians is to reflect Jesus – more of Jesus and less of ourselves.

When you enter the place of rest in green pastures and by quiet waters with the Lord, arrive with joy, and expect to leave with peace: "He makes me to lie down in green pastures; He leads me beside the still waters. He restores my soul" (Psalms 23:2). Expect therefore to be refreshed and restored after spending time with the Lord.

When you are beside quiet waters in the presence of the Lord, His Spirit also gives freedom: "Now the Lord is the Spirit; and where the Spirit of the Lord is, there is liberty" (2 Corinthians 3:17). There is peace of mind and freedom in His presence. Take the time to lock yourself away with the Lord, and get to know Him more in your relationship by communicating with Him, not only talking but also taking the time to listen. The Lord is always talking to us; we just need to take time out and listen to His still small voice as His Spirit speaks to our hearts.

Have you ever taken the time to sit by a river or a lake, maybe watching the swans float by, just beholding the beauty of God's handywork all around you? Do you recall the peace and calmness of that moment? Or when you can hear the birds chirping or the squirrels cracking pine nuts, or hear and see the wind blowing gently through the leaves of the trees – what an awesome way to enjoy the beauty of our Creator. In the same way, it is good to truly take the time to bask in the presence of the Lord.

The Lord will always give us direction for our lives, and when we rise early to pray, He may even give us a warning about things to look out for throughout the day, and instruct us on how to deal with these situations.

God is wonderful; He cares for His children and will never lead us down the wrong path. He is our Heavenly Father, looking out for us and giving us wise council. It's up to us to obey Him and when we do just that, we will reap the rewards of being faithful and obedient to our father. There are many things in this world that try to offer a sense of direction. Everything the Lord knew we had the need for has already been prepared for us, and the way out of our darkest situations has already been paid for on the cross of Calvary. We have access to everything God has promised us in His Word. He has done His part and now it's time for us to do ours.

Jesus tells us to come to Him and He will give us rest from the pain of our weary soul: "Come to Me, all you who labor and are heavy laden, and I will give you rest" (Matthew 11:28). All it takes is a step of faith towards Him and to simply allow Him to hold you in His presence where you can enjoy His fullness of joy. If you are finding your life full of unrest and constant worry, you need to renew your mind with the love of God, and by thinking of those things that are of a good report.

God wants us to be in a place of freedom and everlasting joy, and as we meditate on His Word and apply it to our lives, we will walk in the confidence of the Lord and have good success.

Security and stability are qualities that most people seek and can only really be found in having a relationship with our Lord, Jesus Christ. Having knowledge of God's Word is a great asset to our existence and this also dictates the joy and peace that will surround our lives.

By Standing on God's Word you will find stability, along with peace and joy. Just trust in the Lord for He keeps His promises. He is always looking out for your best, just as a good father would.

CHAPTER 12
Moving Forward

> "Brethren, I count not myself to have apprehended; but this one thing I do, forgetting those things which are behind, and reaching forth unto those things which are before, I press toward the mark for the prize of the high calling of God in Christ Jesus" (Philippians 3:13-14).

Keep your eyes on Jesus, and stay focused on Him. It's time to stop looking backward, and move forward in the Lord. In order for the Lord to lock the doors to your past, you must first forgive yourself and others. Don't allow yourself to hold onto the painful memories. Just let the Lord free you from the guilt and the shame. It's not always easy to forgive, but it's an absolute must if you expect to move forward in your life. Only then will you be able to enjoy the wonderful blessings that the Lord has in store for you. The Word of God says: "For if you forgive men their trespasses, your heavenly Father will also forgive you. But if you do not forgive men their trespasses, neither will your Father forgive your trespasses (Matthew 6:14-15). At times it's hard to forgive, but I guarantee you that once you do forgive yourself and others, your life will be transformed.

You will be free in your spirit, and he who the son sets free is truly free indeed (John 8:36).

It is better to move forward in the Lord than to look back.

> ...bearing with one another, and forgiving one another, if anyone has a complaint against another; even as Christ forgave you, so you also must do. But above all these things put on love, which is the bond of perfection. And let the peace of God rule in your hearts, to which also you were called in one body; and be thankful.
> (Colossians 3:13-15)

Here we are reminded once again to forgive as we were forgiven and also to be thankful in all things.

The Lord always has a way of turning the storms in our lives around for His glory.

In Genesis 50:19-21, Joseph extends mercy to his brothers who meant to harm him:

> Joseph said to them, "Do not be afraid, for am I in the place of God? But as for you, you meant evil against me; but God meant it for good, in order to bring it about as it is this day, to save many people alive. Now therefore, do not be afraid; I will provide for you and your little ones."

Oftentimes in scripture, what was meant for evil, God turned it around for the good of many.

Now it is time for the sun to shine in your life once more; the storm is over now, and you can smile again. Don't let your disappointments consume you; this will only become a hindrance to your walk with God. We all like to use the expression 'spring cleaning' when it comes to cleaning our home for the spring season. In the same way, it is good to allow the Lord to clean us up, and take out all the clutter of our past. He is the best one to do the deep cleaning of our wounded soul. The Lord will remove the cob webs and throw out the garbage from our minds and our spirits; we cannot do this by ourselves. Just let Him refresh your spirit, and you will be ready to accomplish the will of God for your life.

You will also be able to take care of others, but first take care of yourself. This is not selfishness; it is letting the Lord restore you so you can help others along the way.

Endure to the end; there is no deliverance in turning back. When the Lord says it's time to move forward, just do so in the power of His might, and He Himself will open doors for you: "I know thy works: behold, I have set before thee an open door, and no man can shut it: for thou hast a little strength, and hast kept my word, and hast not denied my name" (Revelation 3:8 KJV).

There is a test of endurance and the prize at the end of the challenge should be what we work towards. Life here on earth is a race so we must all press towards the finish line, which is our heavenly home. We all face obstacles in our lives, and there are distractions all around us, but the important thing is to keep our eyes on the prize, and stay focused. Stay on track and you won't lose. We as believers are challenged to run and to win the race. There is no defeat in God; He did not create us to lose. His intention is for us to be victorious. So while running this race called life, we need to lay aside every baggage of the past that would hold us back from moving forward, because we all have a purpose and a calling to be fulfilled. If you allow pain to stay in your heart, it will destroy you, and your destiny.

You may feel alone at times but Jesus is with you. And a good way to truly change your situation is through prayer. Your prayer can and will take the pain of the past away; the truth is that only God can fix the things you are going through. Trust Him. You see, it makes no sense to worry and fret because we already have the victory through the blood of the Lamb. God knows best what the heart needs; He is our Creator.

God is the best friend you could ever have. He knows everything about you, so when you are feeling lonely, just remember that you are not alone. The

Lord is right there, not only at your side but also in your heart. His power can and will transform you and your situation, and your life will never be the same.

Be thankful unto God and bless His name, for the Lord is faithful. Whatever God has said, He will do it; He always keeps His promises.

> So shall My word be that goes forth from My mouth;
> It shall not return to Me void,
> But it shall accomplish what I please,
> And it shall prosper in the thing for which I sent it.
> (Isaiah 55:11)

When you are free from what was holding you in bondage, you will get where you need to be in this life; and remember your ultimate destiny is heaven bound. So while living this life, keep heaven in sight. While you do this, lay aside every distraction and weight that can hinder you in where you want to go. Keep in mind that you are in the hands of the Almighty God, and He has the ability to chip off all that holds you back, causing you to move into victory.

Our Creator has designed for us to succeed, to run the race and to win the race. You are a winner, so have a winning attitude. We are precious clay in the hands of the potter, and God is constantly molding us and shaping us for success.

Sometimes we have areas in our lives that need to be made over, and it's so good when one can truly look and examine his or her life and see where they can do better, because no matter how far God brings us, there is always room for improvement.

Just take a moment to examine and meditate on the areas in your life that may need improvement. One of the things I just love about God is that, even though He already knows everything about us, He takes pleasure when we talk and commune with him.

Being a Christian has nothing to do with religion. Religion is man-made. A true Christian is one who has a personal relationship with God – the God who wakes us up each morning. His very blood runs through our veins; He is the life that keeps our heart pumping. He is not only the Higher Power – all power also belongs to God. He is God alone; none other is fit to take heaven's throne. He is the King of kings and the Lord of lords.

> Thus says the Lord, your Redeemer,
> And He who formed you from the womb:
> "I am the Lord, who makes all things,
> Who stretches out the heavens all alone,
> Who spreads abroad the earth by Myself."
> (Isaiah 44:24)

There are many scriptures that confirm just who God is, and the more you study, the more you will understand God and His Word. Spend quality time in the presence of the Lord – in prayer, in praise, in worship, and of course, in His Word. Remember who you are and whose you are. Just have faith, believe, and run this race with patience. Live your life while keeping your eyes on heaven.

Patience is a vital attribute to our existence in society as well as our walk with God, and we must be patient with others as God is patient with us. The pleasures of this life are temporal but everything pertaining to the Spirit of God is eternal. Patience will enable you to go through the tough storms of affliction with God carrying you through. You are victorious; It is written time and again that nothing is too hard for God (Genesis 18:14; Jeremiah 32:17; Jeremiah 32:27). What seems impossible to man is possible with God (Matthew 19:26; Matthew 10:27; Luke 1:37; Luke 18:27). Good practice comes when you are in fellowship daily with God. Every day comes with its challenges, for Satan will not rest; he is constantly plotting and planning to see you fall. Nonetheless, simply keep your eyes on Jesus, remembering that you have more power than the enemy does. Just don't be ignorant to his devices.

For though we walk in the flesh, we do not war according to the flesh. For the weapons of our warfare are not carnal but mighty in God for pulling down strongholds, casting down arguments and every high thing that exalts itself against the knowledge of God, bringing every thought into captivity to the obedience of Christ."
(2 Corinthians 10:3-6)

The Lord will always answer the cry of His people, and what pleases Him is when we worship Him in spirit and in truth every day. Live a life of total obedience to God; He will do great things for you.

God is about to bless you. In order to live out the blessings, you must speak words of faith, stay focused and on track.

There are things that we need to leave behind us in order to move forward. When you are thinking of the goodness of Jesus in your life, your mind is to stay there. Think and meditate on those things. God has picked us up and cleaned us off. No matter what you have lost in life, know that there is something greater to gain. Again, live your life with eternity in sight. Ultimately, the most important thing to know is what we need to do to get to heaven.

Yet while we are here on earth, we have all been given a mandate to subdue and take dominion over the earth. God has left the things in this life in our care: "Then God said, 'Let Us make man in Our image, according to Our likeness; let them have dominion over the fish of the sea, over the birds of the air, and over the cattle, over all the earth and over every creeping thing that creeps on the earth'" (Genesis 1:26). God has placed us in a position of authority to take care of His creation.

God has also given us insight as to how we should live. Furthermore, He foretold us of the things we would have to endure while we go through this life: "These things I have spoken to you, that in Me you may have peace. In the world you will have tribulation; but be of good cheer, I have overcome the world" (John 16:33). In Christ Jesus we have peace; this is why it is good to set our affections on things above and remain positive about the outcome of it all.

Don't allow the enemy to shift you from your position of destiny, for your mandate must be completed. Just stand firm on the Word of God. You have been positioned by God to affect change – at work, at school, in your community and wherever you go in this world. We are children of the Lord. Our life is subject to His will, and God expects of us to make a difference in our surroundings, just as Jesus did: "how God anointed Jesus of Nazareth with the Holy Spirit and with power, who went about doing good and healing all who were oppressed by the devil, for God was with Him" (Acts 10:38). Take your position and

God given right, and exercise the gift that is within you. Be brave, bold and strong in the Lord; you belong to the great kingdom of God. Think like the champion you are and believe that you will walk in victory in every situation. Your position in life is one that is above only and not below (Deuteronomy 28:13); let nothing stop or slow you down in your tracks.

Silence the enemy in your life by focusing on the words and promises you have received from God. Take your calling and gifting seriously, for lives and souls are waiting in the balance to be saved; they are waiting to hear your testimony. Souls are longing to hear the song in your heart, the music from your instrument, to read your poems of deliverance and the words in your book as you share you testimony. Through your gifting, souls will be ministered to and delivered by the anointing and power of God.

Continue on in the faith for there is much work to be done, and remember that you have to go through it, whatever the "it" may be, in order to come out. The solution to every problem is *Jesus*. So let your prayers go up before God as a sweet-smelling aroma (Ephesians 5:2). There is no excuse not to live a life of prayer, and no matter where you are in your life, you can cry out to the Lord and He will hear and answer you. Just believe God and that He is able. God is sovereign; He is the one who put in order the elements of this world, and He created everything to obey Him, even humankind. So why do we fight against His will at times? He knows what's best for us. And the good desires of our heart, He already knows them, because He is the one who placed them there.

One of my desires is to have a long life, so that I may be able by the grace and mercy of God to accomplish the mission He has sent me upon this earth to fulfill. Nothing gives me more joy than serving my Heavenly Father. Passion is truly a driving force that pushes us to go on living, and by God's grace, enables us to survive the rampant storms of life that come our way. Be brave and strong knowing that every storm only makes you stronger and causes you to persevere in the hardest of times.

We as children of God are encouraged to look to the Lord in times of need or trouble, for this is where our help comes from – day and night. Our Lord never sleeps nor fails to come through for us.

> I will lift up my eyes to the hills—
> From whence comes my help?
> My help comes from the Lord,
> Who made heaven and earth.
> He will not allow your foot to be moved;

He who keeps you will not slumber.
Behold, He who keeps Israel
Shall neither slumber nor sleep.
The Lord is your keeper;
The Lord is your shade at your right hand.
The sun shall not strike you by day,
Nor the moon by night.
The Lord shall preserve you from all evil;
He shall preserve your soul.
The Lord shall preserve your going out and your coming in
From this time forth, and even forevermore.
(Psalms 121:1-8)

Lord, help us to move forward in our lives and always turn to you for help.

Do not remember the former things,
Nor consider the things of old.
Behold, I will do a new thing,
Now it shall spring forth;
Shall you not know it?
I will even make a road in the wilderness
And rivers in the desert.
(Isaiah 43:18-19)

CHAPTER 13
Find Your Place in God

Some people do not realize they have abilities. There are those who feel they are absolutely worthless and have nothing to offer God and others.

If this is you, now is the time to break out of your shell, and use your God given abilities or talents to help and encourage others.

Some of us may be hindered by a false sense of humility about our abilities. If you were to give someone a gift, how would you feel if the person denied it or even pretended that they had never received it in the first place? Surely you would not be pleased. In the same way, God certainly isn't pleased when we hide our abilities, as we have seen in the parable of the talents (read Matthew 24:14-30). He expects us to perfect the talents He has given us and to use them for His glory.

Some people may not appreciate the abilities God has given them. To these folks, the talents of others often seem more desirable than their own. So instead of developing their own special gifts, they sometimes attempt to adopt the talents of others, with disastrous results. Such people fail on two counts: they have neglected their own abilities and in all likelihood have not successfully imitated their idol.

Then there are those who, because they do not possess a particular desired ability, will not attempt anything for God. Let us not despise the smallest ability God puts in us.

Many people who are used by the Lord are the ones no one pays attention to, and they feel insignificant. But watch out, for these same individuals are the ones the Lord is using to do a great work in His kingdom. So we must be very careful how we treat one another, for we could be putting down the next great poet, song writer, missionary, pastor, bishop, deacon, choir director, teacher, and so on.

Some may have a misconception of what a talent is. I believe most of us, if we were asked what comes to mind when we hear the word talent, would probably refer to something along the lines of singing or playing an instrument. Unfortunately, musical skill is all some people associate with talent. However, talent includes more than being able to sing a song or play a tune. Talent is any natural ability that can be cultivated by the one possessing it.

Some people are unwilling to let God use their abilities because of their desire for personal gain. The worldly individual reasons that it is more profitable to invest their talents in the world system than in the kingdom of God. The Bible reads:

> For the love of money is a root of all kinds of evil, for which some have strayed from the faith in their greediness, and pierced themselves through with many sorrows. But you, O man of God, flee these things and pursue righteousness, godliness, faith, love, patience, gentleness. Fight the good fight of faith, lay hold on eternal life, to which you were also called and have confessed the good confession in the presence of many witnesses.
> (1 Timothy 6:10-12)

The love of money, fame, and power has caused many people to squander their talents on temporal things. But the wise man heeds to the words of Jesus:

> "Do not lay up for yourselves treasures on earth, where moth and rust destroy and where thieves break in and steal; but lay up for yourselves treasures in heaven, where neither moth nor rust destroys and where thieves do not break in and steal."
> (Matthew 6:19-20)

We must exercise proper stewardship of our abilities and talents. It is good for us to take inventory of our abilities – to know what they are. Some of us may possess hidden talents, or talents that are rusty from years of neglect. We should ask God to show us what special abilities we possess. Many times neither we nor those around us recognize the potential that lies within us. We are to make our talents available for God's use. A pastor once said that the greatest ability is availability. As long as we make ourselves available to God, He will enable us in greater ways. The Bible has many examples of people who accomplished great things for God, not only through their outstanding abilities, but simply because they were willing to let God use the abilities they had. Consider Moses, for example. Because he was willing to serve, God used his training and background to win a mighty deliverance for the children of Israel. God will use us too, if our heart's cry is, "*Jesus, use me!*" We should make definite plans to further develop and improve our abilities. Improving our abilities is not out of order, for God is not pleased with unfaithful service.

The psalmist David said to the musicians to play *skillfully* with a loud noise (Psalms 33:3). It is a good thing for us to want to be the very best we can be for God, and making good use of the talents and gifts He has given us.

CHAPTER 14
Rejoice in the Lord Always

"Now may the God of hope fill you with all joy and peace in believing, that you may abound in hope by the power of the Holy Spirit" (Romans 15:13).

When you read the title of this book, *Wounded Soul Rejoice*, you might be saying to yourself, "What does rejoicing have to do with a wounded soul?" I'll admit that it is hard sometimes to smile through the pain. And when you get to that place where you can forgive those who have harmed you, it's also important that you forgive yourself as well, so that you may fully move on with your life after the hurtful ordeal. You can only accomplish this by casting all our cares upon the Lord. Please let Him fight your battles for you. He is able to keep you and see you through. Just be encouraged, keep your head up and look to heaven – where your help comes from.

With forgiveness comes the peace of God, the peace that passes all understanding (Philippians 4:7), and since Jesus is an overcomer, well so are you.

When you have a forgiving heart, the Lord will be able to take you higher, and ultimately show the world that the devil is a liar. Our prayer should be, *"Lord fix my heart, that I may be used by you."* The Lord wants to change your heart so that you may be free to rejoice and praise the Lord. When you are in the presence of Almighty God, He will bless you and you will remain blessed.

It's a sad reality that there are those who are not interested in growing in the Lord. Don't be concerned with what's happening around you, for the enemy of your soul just wants to distract you from fulfilling your purpose in this life. No matter what you are going through, rejoice in the Lord, always – through the good times and the hard times.

Even if we have been wounded in some way, we have so much to give thanks for – even to rejoice about – through all our tribulations, and it is beyond human comprehension. The joy of the Lord is our strength (Nehemiah 8:10), and through it all we learn to trust in God and to depend upon His Word. When we call upon the name of the Lord Jesus, something must happen, and when we have the Holy Spirit, we are able to discern the spirits that are contrary to the Word of God. When you are rooted in the Word of the living God, you will stand up for the truth without any doubt.

As you walk with the Lord, trials will come to test your faith, but don't faint; trust in God. Numbers 10:10 reads, "Also in the day of your gladness, in your appointed feasts, and at the beginning of your months, you shall blow the trumpets over your burnt offerings and over the sacrifices of your peace offerings; and they shall be a memorial for you before your God: I am the Lord your God." In Psalms 30:11-12, it is written:

> You have turned for me my mourning into dancing;
> You have put off my sackcloth and clothed me with gladness,
> To the end that my glory may sing praise to You and not be silent.
> O Lord my God, I will give thanks to You forever.

Jesus is sweeter than anything I know; I will tell of His goodness wherever I go.

All the wounds and scars we've attained through the years, God has a purpose for, and all our experiences, weather good or bad, was to make us stronger and to prepare us for our destiny. Don't give up hope, for there is hope in Christ Jesus.

We all have a choice to do right or wrong, and there are consequences when we do wrong, but there is a greater feeling of fulfilment when we do what is right, for God created us that way. Remember the good acts of love you committed the other day, or the prayers you prayed for that one needy soul? Well, the Bible says that what you did in secret will be rewarded to you openly by God (Matthew 6:1-5).

I have found throughout my journey that the best way to confuse the enemy is to praise God with all my heart. When I was going through my healing process, the devil really thought he had me, but I decided to give him a knockout every time. Praise and worship became a part of my every day schedule, and still is today. There is always a song in my heart; even when I sleep at times, I can hear a song from the Lord in my spirit and I know that He has placed it there for a reason.

Through your praise you're also going through a deliverance process, because your mind is no longer on the problem, but rather steadfast upon the problem-solver. There is nothing too hard for God, His love for us is everlasting and He inhabits the praises of His people (Psalms 22:3).

I love the Lord and I won't take it back for He has been so good to me. The devil thought he had me but Jesus came right on time, to rescue me from the plan of darkness. I have learned to love and serve the Lord with all my heart and talk to the storms in my life, commanding them to go, in Jesus' name.

As you go about your day, walk in the love of God. Do everything in love and allow the joy of the Lord to strengthen you.

I am sure we have all experienced working with or simply being around people who are hard to get along with; every day, they seem to have something to complain about. They seem miserable and without joy. I've come to understand that these people don't have the joy of the Lord, and we who are blessed enough to have it are to share it. I believe that just like laughter is contagious, so is joy.

As I go about my day, I purposely smile and say hello to everyone in my path. Even if I see someone in a gloomy mood, I try to cheer them up, because when I think of the goodness of the Lord and all He has done for me, there is always joy in heart.

If we would just take the time to reflect on God's goodness towards us and give Him thanks at all times, we would get through each day with inner joy no matter what the struggle is. The Lord knows that in this life, situations get us down and that's just our human reality. The key is not to let life get you down but to put your trust in the Almighty God, for He carried the weight of the world on His shoulders so that we wouldn't have to. Hold your chin up, cheer up, and look up to the sky, knowing that there is hope for a better tomorrow.

Let's live in the joy of knowing that God loves us more than we could ever imagine. There is so much that we can give God thanks for. He woke us up this morning and even now, He is keeping us through the day. Just look at what the Lord has done and what He is doing. Give thanks for the air you breathe, for your health, for your family… the list goes on and on.

You can rejoice and rest assured knowing that no matter what, your needs will be met by the Lord, your provider.

"And my God shall supply all your need according to His riches in glory by Christ Jesus" (Philippians 4:19).

CHAPTER 15
Pray, Believe and Without Fail, Recover All

Through prayer, we shall recover all. Faith is also crucial to our very survival in this walk with the Lord. Let God fulfill His purpose. Faith touches God's willingness to work on our behalf; faith in God definitely makes things happen. The Lord will work according to our faith.

Your faith and trust in God will trigger miracles to come forth in your life. But you cannot trust God unless you know who He is. Get to know God by reading the scriptures and pray according to His promises; then trust that God will answer your prayers. Get to know about His power and ability because when you do, it will be easier to trust in Him. God is able to provide for you even in the face of adversity; don't give up on God for He won't give up on you.

The walls of Jericho fell down flat because the people trusted God and gave Him a shout:

> So the people shouted when the priests blew the trumpets. And it happened when the people heard the sound of the trumpet, and the people shouted with a great shout, that the wall fell down flat. Then the people went up into the city, every man straight before him, and they took the city.

(Joshua 6:20)

Trust and believe God for all things. Let us imitate the faith of the three Hebrew boys who never lost their faith, even when faced with the fiery furnace with no sign of God showing up to save them (Daniel 3:8-18).

We are called to live out the purpose of our existence on earth. While there is time, let us seek God. Faith does not rely on logic or proof. True faith is in seeking God, when we believe without seeing it in the natural realm, knowing that all things are possible with God.

God desires to have a personal relationship with mankind. We need to put our faith and trust in Him for only He can bring about liberty. No one can be free from the bondage of Satan unless they rely on God. Dependency on God will bring about peace, joy, liberty, freedom and everything that is good in life.

Prayer is hard work; however without prayer, we become weak. We need to be in the presence of God to be filled with His spirit, and His anointing. As the Bible says, we are to "pray without ceasing" (1 Thessalonians 5:17). Prayer moves the hand of God and grants us His favor. Payer brings revelation of ourselves; the Lord will show us what needs to be changed in our lives. Prayer causes us to totally depend on God. Just like the potter, the Lord knows the potential of the lump of clay. God will hold us when we allow Him to; this is why we must yield ourselves to Him.

Obedience is a great part of our prayer life, for at times the Lord may even wake us up out of our sleep to intercede on behalf of someone else. For example, one night while sleeping, I had a dream that my oldest nephew was walking away from a yellow school bus. He was wearing his school uniform at that time, but was not going on the bus; and the dream ended just like that. At that time in my nephew's life, he was not going to school and started not coming home. It was about 5:00 a.m. when the Lord woke me up from this dream and instructed me to pray for him. To my great surprise that same day, my nephew went back home to his mother's house and started attending school again. If I did not wake up to pray that morning, there is no telling where he would be today. Why live with this regret?

When God puts a burden in your spirit to pray for someone it usually should be done right away, for the Lord can bring deliverance even at that very moment. We must cease every opportunity to be used by the Lord, for He is always looking for someone that He can use to bless a wounded soul. We are all precious in His sight.

Prayer will also keep you from turning cold or worse yet, turning away from the Lord. He who kneels before God will stand, especially in times of trouble.

Another great benefit of prayer is that it helps us govern our actions and control our mouths – keeping us from doing or saying things that we would later regret.

Furthermore, a person who prays before reading the Bible will better understand the Word of God, for prayer brings about spiritual understanding and wisdom. It's also good to ask God for wisdom, as it is written in James 1:5-6:

If any of you lacks wisdom, let him ask of God, who gives to all liberally and without reproach, and it will be given to him. But let him ask in faith, with no doubting, for he who doubts is like a wave of the sea driven and tossed by the wind. But let him ask in faith, nothing wavering.

Wisdom is what allows us to apply what we know properly. Let's try never making an important decision without praying first. God does not want us to fail. He wants to direct us every step of the way.

The battle is not yours but belongs to the Lord, and when Christ is in your life there is no need to fear: "The Lord is my light and my salvation; whom shall I fear? The Lord is the strength of my life; of whom shall I be afraid?" (Psalms 27:1 KJV) The Lord speaks to His prophet in Isaiah 41:10 KJV, saying, "Fear thou not; for I am with thee: be not dismayed; for I am thy God: I will strengthen thee; yea, I will help thee; yea, I will uphold thee with the right hand of my righteousness." Again, when you think that you're alone, God is with you, and He knows what you need to be sharpened, to be made strong.

God is always in full control. Some people may not think so, especially with all the things happening in the world today, but as believers we know that there is a purpose and reason for everything. We also know that God has given us free will and authority on this earth, and He needs our prayers.

Our Lord is victorious; He will work everything out for our good. Even after we've been through the fire, He will cause us to come out as pure gold. Therefore, put your faith in God; He is going to work it out. Just say, *"I will trust in God!"* Keep praying, keep believing, and He will see you through it all. Proverbs 3:5-6 reads:

> Trust in the Lord with all your heart,
> And lean not on your own understanding;
> In all your ways acknowledge Him,
> And He shall direct your paths.

Psalms 37:3-5 gives another powerful example of trusting God with faith that He will come through:

> Trust in the Lord, and do good;
> Dwell in the land, and feed on His faithfulness.
> Delight yourself also in the Lord,
> And He shall give you the desires of your heart.
> Commit your way to the Lord,
> Trust also in Him,
> And He shall bring it to pass.

You are strong when Christ is in your life, and you will always have the victory. You will win spiritual battles with Jesus on your side; just know where to find your strength. Remember that the joy of the Lord is our strength. Everything you go through, just turn it over to Jesus Christ. Hold your head up high, walk with confidence in the Lord, for Jesus never fails. There is a reward when you have confidence in God.

God has a plan for your life; live in obedience to His will. After you have been obedient, then you shall receive the promise. This was the case for Job in the book of Job 42:10: "And the Lord restored Job's losses when he prayed for his friends. Indeed the Lord gave Job twice as much as he had before." Therefore, even though you have been wounded, trust that God has a plan to bless you when you remain faithful through even the most painful seasons.

Think yourself happy, for you have the victory through Christ Jesus. We see the Apostle Paul do this in Acts 26:1-2; "So Paul stretched out his hand and answered for himself: 'I think myself happy, King Agrippa, because today I shall answer for myself before you concerning all the things of which I am accused by the Jews.'" Do as Paul did and encourage yourself through every situation life may throw at you. Remember the One who brings fullness of joy; focus on the problem-solver rather than the problem. When I think of the goodness of Jesus, and all He's done for me, my soul cries out, *"Hallelujah! Thank you God for saving me."*

All God needs is one opportunity to move in your heart, and I guarantee you that He will change the state of your heart and your life in the process. When you have faith and trust in God, He'll open doors of opportunity that you thought could never be possible.

The Lord will reveal His will to you, and it's up to you to grab ahold of it. Be confident in your calling. When God reveals it to you, remember that God knows you're the best person for the job, and you don't have to prove anything to anyone, for your gift will follow you and make room for you. There is a process that takes place when you begin to understand that the ideas that come into your spirit are actually from God. He is molding you into the vessel of honor He has created you to be.

No matter the weather, I'm here to let you know that life will get better! Have confidence in God. The Bible describes this confidence as follows: "Now this is the confidence that we have in Him, that if we ask anything according to His will, He hears us. And if we know that He hears us, whatever we ask, we know that we have the petitions that we have asked of Him" (1 John 5:14-15).

The Lord will heal you from your brokenness. Deliverance is for all; it's available for both the victim and the offender. Pray for the healing and deliverance of the individual who has harmed you. In doing this, without fail you shall recover all! We read the following in 1 Samuel 30:6-8:

> Now David was greatly distressed, for the people spoke of stoning him, because the soul of all the people was grieved, every man for his sons and his daughters. But David strengthened himself in the Lord his God. Then David said to Abiathar the priest, Ahimelech's son, "Please bring the ephod here to me." And Abiathar brought the ephod to David. So David inquired of the Lord, saying, "Shall I pursue this troop? Shall I overtake them?" And He answered him, "Pursue, for you shall surely overtake them and without fail recover all."

At times we need to reflect on where our strength comes from. God has given every one of us an anointing and the power to fight. Our strength comes from the Lord, and the devil's plan is to use our weakness to try and conquer our strength. Be strong in the Lord, and don't take your walk with Him lightly.

God is great. His name is above every other name and He is most worthy of our praise. All power and all glory belong to God. When you feel the enemy begin to press on you, press back even harder in the power of Almighty God. Never lose focus on what God has called you to do. Deceit and discouragement is what the enemy will use to get you off track; but stay fixated on God and His Word.

Make it part of your daily routine to encourage yourself in the Lord, and He will guard you and hold you up. Find your secret place in the Lord and know that no matter the problem, God will always come through for you. Don't let your circumstance shift you from the position of authority God Has placed you in.

Also know that God will always provide for those who love Him. Speak the Word of God over your life. Go through the storms and come out stronger and better than you were before. Let the Lord revive and restore you as He speaks to your heart.

I've learned to stop feeling pity for myself, for in my weakness I know God's strength is made perfect.

Even when wrong has been done to us we are to love and pray for one another. The Lord will increase your strength; wait upon the Lord for He never fails.

We may fall but we need to get back up again, forget the things that are behind us, and continue to press forward.

God has already blessed us, and the miracles we are praying for have already been taken care of. We are God's property. We belong to Him completely and the enemy cannot touch us. Once we were in the devil's grip, but now we have been redeemed by the blood of Jesus. So the enemy has no right to touch us – even the grave cannot hold us down. Let's rejoice in God our savior. The devil can never cross the blood line of Jesus Christ, and the angels of the Lord are all around us.

All is well; God is on the throne and He loves you. No matter the problem you are facing today, only believe this is your moment of breakthrough. We are to live our lives in the supernatural where miracles are a normal occurrence. Activate your faith and watch the power of God move in your life, even in the things that seem to be dead.

In the book of John, we read the story of Lazarus whom Jesus raised from the dead after four days in the tomb. Lazarus' sister Martha, when told by Jesus that her brother would be raised from the dead, doubted that this could happen in the physical realm: "Jesus said to her, 'Your brother will rise again.' Martha said to Him, 'I know that he will rise again in the resurrection at the last day'" (John 11:23-24). Imagine a situation like that of Lazarus happening to someone close to you. How would you react? Would you make a statement like Martha or would you have faith in the supernatural power of God?

In this same story, Jesus heard that the one he loved was sick, but "he stayed two more days in the place where he was" (John 11:6). We must all have faith, but at times life's circumstances make it difficult to do so. Most of us say we have faith in God, but do we really trust God with everything that concerns us? The Word of God tells us to cast all our cares upon Him for He cares for us (1 Peter 5:7).

At times we look at our lives and think to ourselves, "What is going on here? Why am I not seeing my faith being manifested in my life?" God is way above our human understanding and we have to allow His Holy Spirit to work faith in our souls. That is why the Bible describes faith as "the evidence of things not seen" (Hebrews 11:1). We can't see in this natural realm the promises that God has in store for us, but in the Bible we can read of the things God has for those who love Him. That's why we need to remember His Word, and prophecy them over our lives, especially in those times when we look around and wonder what is going on. If we can trust God we will see He is faithful. When we don't see the promises of God coming to pass when we want them to, it's good to just take time to reflect on His Word, which will give us the strength to go on. God does not always come through when we want Him to, but He is always on time. *Thank you, Jesus!*

Let's never be at a place where we are telling God what to do. How about simply taking Him at His Word, trusting and love Him with all of our hearts? For there is nothing too hard for God to do for us; He is in the business of restoration.

He will not fail in recovering everything you may have lost. He may do it in unexpected ways, but just hold on to your faith, for it will move the mountains.

CHAPTER 16
See Love through the Eyes of Christ

"If someone says, 'love God,' and hates his brother, he is a liar; for he who does not love his brother whom he has seen, how can he love God whom he has not seen?"
(1 John 4:20)

God is love, and out of love God made us all. We were birthed out of His love. Wherever we go we should reflect the love of God, so that when the world looks at us they see and feel the love that emanates from our being. The scriptures state the following in 1 John 4:7-11:

> Beloved, let us love one another, for love is of God; and everyone who loves is born of God and knows God. He who does not love does not know God, for God is love. In this the love of God was manifested toward us, that God has sent His only begotten Son into the world, that we might live through Him. In this is love, not that we loved God, but that He loved us and sent His Son to be the propitiation for our sins. Beloved, if God so loved us, we also ought to love one another.

It is so important that we portray love to everyone the Lord allows us to come in contact with. The Lord will use us all in different ways to share the love He has placed within us. One of the ways the Lord has inspired me to share love is by writing this book and making it accessible to all.

We can always say that we love someone but as the saying goes, actions speak louder than words. Love is sincere, and merciful, as we read in Ephesians 2:4-6:

> But God, who is rich in mercy, because of His great love with which He loved us, even when we were dead in trespasses, made us alive together with Christ (by grace you have been saved), and raised us up together, and made us sit together in the heavenly places in Christ Jesus...

It is so important for us to understand each other and know that none of us are perfect. Then we will be able to have more patience with one another.

The next time you get angry and you may feel like giving someone a piece of your mind, have compassion instead, and remember that God is not finished with any of us yet! The way we see each other, and the way we see ourselves, is nothing close to how our Heavenly Father sees us. With our human eyes we can only observe what we see naturally. But if we would take the time to get into the deeper things of God – through prayer, praise and worship – He would reveal who we really are in Him.

God sees us as His finished product, the anointed men and women of God that He has created us to be. We may not like what others do at times, but we still need to love them. Love the individual, not the deeds.

Love is not proud, therefore be careful not to be full of yourself. Simply let God elevate you as you humble yourself before Him. Luke 18:14 reads, "I tell you, this man went down to his house justified rather than the other; for everyone who exalts himself will be humbled, and he who humbles himself will be exalted." In the same way, it is also written, "Therefore humble yourselves under the mighty hand of God, that He may exalt you in due time" (1 Peter: 4-5).

It's important for our hearts to be made right before the Lord, and God has empowered us with His Holy Spirit, Who lets us know when something we've done is not right.

Love is giving. Let us give because we love to give. Love is that which is given from the very depths of our hearts. Once we love like this, we will truly be a blessing to those around us. We need to love unconditionally, just as God loves; He is slow to lose patience with us.

Give freely of your time, love, and increase and your life will be full of the goodness of God. When you have a giving spirit, you will give to God and He will take care of you and all your needs. Even those around you will experience the love of the Lord through you and the acts of love you share. The love of God is what makes a difference in you. Also remember that your tithes are holy, and whether you give or not, tithes belong to God. Give and be blessed forevermore! Luke 6:38 reads, "Give, and it will be given to you: good measure, pressed down, shaken together, and running over will be put into your bosom. For with the same measure that you use, it will be measured back to you." And when you give towards the work of the Lord, remember to do so with joy, as it is written in 2 Corinthians 9:7, "So let each one give as he purposes in his heart, not grudgingly or of necessity; for God loves a cheerful giver."

It is also important to have fellowship with other believers, for when we are in one accord, it gives glory to God. In John 13:34-35, we read, "A new commandment I give to you, that you love one another; as I have loved you, that you also love one another. By this all will know that you are My disciples, if you have love for one another."

God expects us to bring forth fruit unto Him. John 15:1-2 reads, "I am the true vine, and My Father is the vinedresser. Every branch in Me that does not bear fruit He takes away; and every branch that bears fruit He prunes, that it may bear more fruit." This is followed by: "You did not choose Me, but I chose you and appointed you that you should go and bear fruit, and that your fruit should remain, that whatever you ask the Father in My name He may give you" (John 15:16). Love comes from growth in God; give Him something to work with, and allow God to have His way in your life. When the Lord blesses us, it's so that we can be a blessing to someone. This causes God to release His prosperity upon our lives, and His plan is to turn us into something beautiful for His glory.

Don't let anyone steal your joy to worship God. True worship causes us to enter into the awesome presence of God. The quality time we spend in worship is important. Haven't you noticed how time just slips by during this moment? Time no longer becomes a factor while in the presence of Almighty God. And the closer we get to the Lord through praise and worship, the more we begin to see how important it is in developing our relationship with the Lord as well as our relationship with others.

Life will always have ups and downs and our attitude during the trying times will bring forth either positive or negative views on the situation. Our attitude will reflect what is in our hearts. When Abraham heard that lot was taken captive in Genesis 14, his automatic response was to go get Lot back, and not only did he have that heart of compassion to get Lot out of that life of bondage, he also gathered other people to help in his rescue mission. And when Abraham heard the bad news he did not complain, he did not gossip, and he certainly did not fear; rather, Abraham depended on God's love to help him figure out a plan of rescue to help his brother Lot.

This is how the Lord wants us to respond when we hear that our brothers and sisters in the Lord are in a place where they need help to get out of the situation they are in – to help them no matter what they are facing in their lives. We should respond in such a way to help bring them to a place of freedom and restoration, whether it be through prayer or a physical action such as financial help or simply being supportive in any way possible. This is true love – when we see and know of others in need and we take it upon ourselves to help them out. Our hearts should be filled with compassion, for this is the way our Heavenly Father looked down upon us and had compassion for us in our sinful state.

We are all called to care for the household of faith as we would care for our own physical relatives and those around us we see are in need. Abraham gives a perfect example of that love and compassion to see Lot free.

Let us be a generation of intercessors that will stand in the gap for our brothers and sisters, being moved to action when we hear that our family is in a difficult situation. Let's follow the example of Abraham and be moved to see lives restored by the renewing power of the Holy Ghost.

Each day, take time to think of how much God loves you. John 3:16 describes this best: "For God so loved the world that He gave His only begotten Son, that whoever believes in Him should not perish but have everlasting life." He sent His Son, Jesus to us to heal us, to restore us, to love us, even when we were not worthy of His love. Meditate on this: there is nothing you could ever do to change God's love towards you. Again, never give up on Jesus, for He will never give up on you, and He is worth more than anything in this entire world. My prayer for you is that you will have a refreshing each day in the love of God, which comes by His sweet Holy Spirit.

A gift is a great thing to receive, and when most people hear that a gift is being given, they tend to get very excited with great anticipation. How much more should we as children of the Most High God get excited about the most precious gift that God has given so freely – the gift of His love, in Jesus Christ.

We have no reason to go through this life feeling down or beaten up by the enemy; rather, let us rise up as soldiers in the body of Christ. We are all called to be great men and women of God. What kind of individuals would we be if we did not go through any hard times? God is making us into the vessels of honor He has designed us to be. When we submit to the Lord then we will experience the peace of the Lord which passes all understanding.

The potter wants to put you back together again. There is a difference between chastening and abuse. God always wants us to be in line with Him and His will for us. He loves us enough to use what we've done to bring forth greatness in us. Thank God for everything you've been through because it has made you who you are today. Where God has brought you today is where He wants you to be at this very moment in your life. We may have our own plans but God has the master plan for our lives.

Obstacles will cause us to react by getting us on our knees. When we are going through the process it's not easy, but God uses these hard times to build our character.

It's also good to understand that God will take someone that everyone threw away, someone people call a 'nobody', and turn that person into a 'somebody' with exceptional value, all for His glory. He will take something seemingly of no worth and turn it into something great.

God will use those who show up even when they are going through a trial. Give God the glory no matter what you are going through. Don't faint in opposition, but endure affliction as a good soldier. For God uses our stumbling blocks to build us a house of glory. Your affliction is really working for you, not against you, because God will take your trials and use them for your good. The more you go through the greater the weight of glory – the bigger our trouble the bigger our weight.

When all is said and done, God will pour out His anointing upon you, and send you out to the masses. You cannot draw people to Christ with spiritual words. People need to be ministered to at a level they will understand. God is love and the best thing you can do when sharing about the Lord, is to share what you have been through, and your experiences of God's love towards you and others close to you.

How about sharing Jesus at your workplace, at your school, at the bus stop, in the grocery store, at the bank, or simply everywhere the opportunity arises itself?

Jesus did not tolerate sinners, however He didn't beat them up; He always had compassion. He is the only God who can and will forgive our sins – the only true wise and living God. The world will know God by our love. God is offended when we treat each other badly. We are to show brotherly love, treat people the way we want to be treated, and when we don't, we are not walking in obedience. We say, "I love you, Lord," but we are also to love everyone with the love of the Lord. The world is drawn to love, so we must always share it. We carry the truth, the true nature of who Jesus Christ is. Jesus went where common people were and He found faithful servants by the sea side – Matthew, Mark and so forth.

If you are a born again Christian, you surely remember the state your life was in when you found God. When the world sees the love we have for one another they will look at us and say, "I want that too." This is the beauty of being set apart. We are not the ordinary, 'everyday' dishes; we are the expensive china in the glass cabinet, set apart to be used at the appointed time.

Each angel has an assignment from God and here they are placed to carry out the will of the Lord. How much more are we, who are made in His image, to fulfill our purpose in God?

When you love through the eyes of Christ, you are able to love and forgive those who you thought were your enemies. You can even look at your violators and just be filled with compassion towards them.

Forgiveness is one of the keys to moving on into a brighter future. While growing up I often heard people saying that it is easy to forgive but not to forget. As a young girl around the age of twelve, I used to really wonder what that meant. But as I entered my teenage years and young adulthood stages, I began to understand the importance of forgiveness.

As I would see my uncles quite often at my mother's home, there was always this wall before me. As long as I knew it was them at the door, I would go into my shell, be lost for words, walk away from the door and tell someone else to go and talk with them. In my world I felt like I needed a sincere apology before I could ever speak or even look at them. I held onto those feelings for most of my life. In my eyes they were never worthy of my love and I held on to that bitterness like it was my comfort blanket. This was until the Lord brought me to the true place of forgiveness.

The Lord said to me, "Evelyn, what if you never get that apology? Are you going to live the rest of your life in bitterness?" And in my heart I knew that I needed to forgive them whole heartedly. Well, it took me a while but I eventually had no choice because the unforgiveness was just eating away at my heart like a disease. And as I matured in the Lord I began to see people through the eyes of Christ. It wasn't easy but it was crucial and worthwhile. In fact, as I was writing just a moment ago, I was able to see my uncle and say, "Hello, Uncle," and he said hello back. As this happened, I felt nothing but the love of God flowing through my veins; I felt a change in the atmosphere, and could sense my uncle's surprise.

This is the love of God, and what it can do. If we ever expect to be forgiven must we not also show the same depth of love and compassion when it comes to forgiving others? And as we forgive others, we must also remember to forgive ourselves. For we at times can still be holding on to hate, bitterness, resentment and anger towards others. Forgiving someone also releases them from their own prison of guilt, and it is always our hope that they ultimately repent and ask God for forgiveness.

Many of us are still holding on to hurts from our past and we only need to let them go and let God have His way in our lives. This is what I've learned from my own experiences. The hardest thing for me to do was to forgive my uncles for the abuse and trauma they caused me. And as I look back at those moments now, I realize that they were merely the instruments of the enemy, for no one in their right mind would look at a young child and have sexual desires for her.

Furthermore, I have reflected on the possibility that they too may have been sexually abused at some time in their lives. So you see, some things are generational and the cycle needs to be broken. Only God's deliverance power can break every curse, every chain of bondage in one's life.

The Lord did say in His Word that He has come to set the captives free. It makes no sense to seek revenge for the injustice that may have been done to you, because all vengeance belongs to God. And when you really think about it, the individuals who brought pain and grief into your life also need healing, deliverance and forgiveness, so why continue to live in anger and bitterness towards them? I am not saying that what may have happened to you in the past does not matter. On the contrary it does matter because in order to be free and enjoy your brighter future, you must deal with the past and not push it under the rug, carrying it to your grave. We were all meant to live and enjoy this wonderful life that the Lord has blessed us with, to live freely and in the joy of the Lord, and to forgive and be forgiven.

Pain that is undealt with, or poorly dealt with, is in my opinion the culprit of destruction and death. I believe this because there are many types of diseases and they all come with pain. One may have pain from past memories, from broken relationships, from life's disappointments and so on that may bring them down; we all have experienced these situations. Each individual deals with pain differently, but it's always better to turn negatives into positives. For example, some people when they are grieving or just going through a hard time in their lives may turn to alcohol, drugs, violence, and the list goes on, but these are never ways that will permanently take away the pain – they are only temporary solutions. In fact these things only add to the pain and often lead people down a very destructive path. One must always get to the root of the matter before any true healing can begin.

I am pretty sure that we all see homeless people just wandering in this life, but have we ever really stopped to talk with them, giving a listening ear? Many times while evangelizing, when I actually took the time to stop and listen to these individuals as they shared their stories, I understood that they had all been through some kind of disappointment in life, some grief, some pain, or some form of hardship that led to their homelessness. Certainly none of them woke up one day wanting to be homeless.

God's love is deeper than the ocean, wider than the sea and as you love through the eyes of Christ, when you really see these individuals, the love and compassion of Christ will overwhelm you, leading you to want to minister to the needs of these hurting people.

I have learned much wisdom from God while evangelizing. Sometimes we believe that just passing by an individual and putting money into their hand or cup or whatever they may have will always do the trick. But have you ever really taken the time to actually buy a homeless person a meal, or even to sit down with them and keep them company? I can guarantee that they would as a result be more apt to listen to what the Lord has to say to them through you, simply because you have met their present need. Homeless people are often in need of a good meal, or simply to be seen; let the love of Christ pour out of your heart into actions of love. They may have no shoes on their feet. Why not buy them a pair? Their clothes may be worn out. If you have the means, why not buy them new ones? They may need a good shampooing or haircut. Why not provide for their current need? Most often, it doesn't take much to make a difference in someone's life.

As I sit here in my home writing this chapter, I realize that I could write hundreds of books, but it is the life-changing power in the Word of God that will affect change in the lives of people. We are the vessels He desires to work through for His purposes, and all the glory goes back to Him. He has blessed us all with gifts, and we are to use them for the greater good. In other words, we are blessed to *bless forward*.

CHAPTER 17
The Beauty of Holiness

Beauty comes from within; the glory of God glows from the inside out. Whatever God puts His hands on is beautiful and is wonderfully made, which makes us all beautiful and pleasing on the inside. Everything that is good comes from God. We are blessed with heaven's best.

God Himself is decorating us from the inside out, and He sees the finished product. Life is a journey and so it is when we walk with the Lord. We are a product of holiness which starts on the inside. Purpose in your heart to change into all God has called you to be. Tell Him, *"Lord, you are the potter and I am the clay. Mold me and make me after your will."*

Even when you've lost everything, the Lord will never leave you nor forsake you. The love of God will surpass everything that you have been through, for the Lord has taken away all of our iniquities. Our lives are now hidden in Christ Jesus, and each day we draw closer to our destiny.

Walking with the Lord takes sacrifice, and we must be willing to give up some of the pleasures of this life to surrender and serve the Lord in the beauty of holiness.

The Word of God is like a wardrobe, in which we will find every style, or every Word that is fitting. Have you ever been to the mall and found a nice piece of clothing, only to be disappointed by that label that reads, "one size fits all" when in reality, it doesn't? Well in the case of God's wardrobe, one size always fits all. What a beautiful analogy, for every word fits us perfectly, as well as individually, which brings me to the realization that with God, there is no partiality. There is no partiality when it comes to God, for He has something in store for us all and loves us all just the same. He wants every one of us to shine for Jesus, but He will use us in different situations, communities and countries for His gospel to spread throughout the whole world, for every soul is precious in His sight.

God loves us even when He disapproves of the things we do wrong. *Thank you, Lord for your mercy towards us!*

We can always find a Word that fits us, especially in the situations and trials that we go through. In the trying times, look at the Lord and His attitude and character. Line yourself up with His Word and you will be blessed and better. Keep your integrity and continue to stand on the promises of God.

Your walk with the Lord is not a popularity contest; you don't have to be liked by everyone. Oftentimes when you are, it means you are compromising somewhere. Remember that it is the pure in heart that shall see God (Matthew 5:8). When you walk in holiness (with the Lord) He will lead you beside green pastures. Rest in God; roll all your cares over to Him. Find the green pasture and lie down. Let His Holy Spirit stir up the waters, causing fresh blessings to flow out. Look into the face of your shepherd and keep your eyes on Jesus. As you look towards the shepherd, He will make a way for you. As long as you walk with the Lord, everything is going to be alright.

The Lord is the only thirst quencher. When you drink from His fountain you will never be the same, for God will refresh your life. People are trying to find the fountain of youth when God is the only one who can preserve your life. And when you put your trust in the Almighty God, He will do just that and much more. Remember, we are all beautiful, and because we are re-born of His Spirit, we are renewed daily!

In Hebrews 12:14-15, we read: "Pursue peace with all people, and holiness, without which no one will see the Lord: looking carefully lest anyone fall short of the grace of God; lest any root of bitterness springing up cause trouble, and by this many become defiled." The fight is on for us to be more like God. Walking in His footsteps, the evil one is set out to destroy us, but God has come to give us life and also

His Spirit to help us fight off every temptation of the flesh. We should never seek an alternative way when God does not answer right away; remember that God is always on time.

As you move forward in the beauty of holiness, don't remember what God has forgotten. He is a God of newness, and He has made you brand new. The Lord will restore every year the enemy has stolen from you. This can only be done by the supernatural power of God.

CHAPTER 18
The Life Changing Power of God

God gives us power to fight off temptations; we are more than conquerors! In order for this to be our reality, we must not only be hearers but also doers of what God says in His Word (James 1:22-24). The Lord is the only one who can sanctify us from all unrighteousness and make us great, turning us into vessels of honor (2 Timothy 2:20-22).

When you are a born again Christian, you are a new creature in Christ, and God does not look at what we have done in the past. He is our very Creator and sees us as finished products of greatness. We read in 2 Corinthians 5:17, "Therefore, if anyone is in Christ, he is a new creation; old things have passed away; behold, all things have become new."

Witnessing to Lost Souls

It is also of important that we find out what our calling and purpose is in this present life and fulfill our God given ministry: "But you be watchful in all things, endure afflictions, do the work of an evangelist, fulfill your ministry" (2 Timothy 4-5). In 1 Peter 3:15, we read, "But sanctify the Lord God in your hearts, and always be ready to give a defense to everyone who asks you a reason for the hope that is in you, with meekness and fear." Remember that we are all servants of the Lord, and we are to be obedient to His call. So go ahead and introduce each lost sheep to your Heavenly Father, and they will come to know Him by your testimony. Someone took the time to lead you to the Lord, and now is your turn to do the same – to let the world know that Jesus saves!

By the grace of God and through my own personal experiences, I've learned how to be effective in witnessing. The more we learn the more we will share.

I remember on my 16th birthday, a lady at church invited my family over to her house for dinner after Sunday service. She had prepared a variety of food and my eldest brother, my mother and I had such a good time of fellowship at the home. As we sat and enjoyed each other's company, I had such joy in my heart and it amazed me at how kind this woman was to open her home and just be a blessing to us, especially to me. She really took the time to make sure I had an enjoyable time, and I appreciated that so much that I will never forget her kindness. So after we ate the delicious meal she prepared, she asked me if I wanted some desert; and of course my answer was, "Yes, please!" It was homemade cheesecake, and the lady was not sure I would like it since it was her first time making that kind of cake. As I took my first bite, the texture was so rich and smooth. I had never tasted anything like it. When I was done I had to have another serving! This was my first time having cheese cake, and to this very day it is my favorite treat.

This story is simply an example of the seemingly small seeds we plant along the way. We sometimes will never know what the outcome will be; our job is to simply sow according to the Word of God and be a good example of His love in the lives of the people around us. This is wonderfully described in 1 Corinthians 3:6-9:

> I planted, Apollos watered, but God gave the increase. So then neither he who plants is anything, nor he who waters, but God who gives the increase. Now he who plants and he who waters are one, and each one will receive his own reward according to his own labor. For we are God's fellow workers; you are God's field, you are God's building."

We are blessed to bless others – it's a chain reaction. The gospel of Christ Jesus is the good news that is to be shared with all. Those who will take the time to receive it with gladness will live in the blessings God has prepared for us all. Since I met Jesus my life has never been the same. God being the potter, He sees the cracks and the chips in our vessels that only He can repair, and that's what He does in us. There is always room for improvement in our lives. The wonderful thing is that the

Lord looks beyond all our faults and still supplies our needs.

When the Spirit of the Lord takes ahold of your life, the evidence can clearly be seen. When you accept the Lord into your heart, you begin to think, dress and act differently, for you begin to understand whose you are and just how precious you are to Jesus.

I've personally come to know the Church as the body of Christ, and with our bodies being His temple we worship the Father in spirit and in truth. Now the physical church building is a spiritual hospital; folks are there to receive inward healing and to hear a message of hope, for this is our daily bread. This is where countless lives are being renewed by the power of the Holy Spirit. The church is also a place where you can meet the Lord Jesus Christ, and when His spirit dwells in you, He is with you forevermore.

How do I know that God is not dead? I know He is alive for His spirit dwells in me, and I can feel Him in my spirit. This is something that changes you from the inside out.

Once you have experienced the transformative power of God, you naturally begin to walk in love, because God is love. You learn to forgive your enemies and your life becomes governed by compassion.

When you allow God to have His way in you, you will begin to know what it means to be free in your spirit, and it is the best feeling in the world when you're able to love again as the scale of unforgiveness is removed from your heart.

I love the Lord so much and this will show in my actions because the love of the Lord flows through my blood stream, through my arteries and through my entire body. Once you experience the Love of God you see the world and everyone in it through the eyes of love.

So allow the Lord to turn your life around and to clothe you in His righteousness. He looks forward to hearing from us each day as we take time to pray and communicate with Him. Our relationship with Him will grow stronger as we give Him space in our daily lives to make us better in all we do. The world will notice that we are different and it will be effortless. Just let your life be an example to those around you and allow the light of God's love to shine through you.

Jesus is alive and full of power and so is His Church, and His power is demonstrated by the move of His Holy Spirit. God want us to be His mouth, hands and feet on this earth, and we have full access to His power by having faith in His name.

If there was ever a time to get closer to God in prayer and through the reading of His Word it is now, because prayer and dedication gets His attention, which causes Him to move in mighty ways. This is not a time for division but a time for the children of God to get together and be a united front in order to win the souls of this world into the kingdom of God. So let us be peacemakers and soul winners for Christ, and show the world the love of God, for there is truly no greater love than the love of God. As it is written, "Greater love has no one than this, than to lay down one's life for his friends" (John 15:13). As a result, we should never be ashamed of the gospel, and what we desire for our family and loved ones we should also desire for those who are lost.

"For I am not ashamed of the gospel of Christ, for it is the power of God to salvation for everyone who believes, for the Jew first and also for the Greek" (Romans 1:16).

CHAPTER 19
True Success

God has called us to success and to accomplish this we must have a healthy relationship with Him. Jesus has fashioned us for greatness, so don't think that because you have been wounded along the way, you are a failure. There is no failure in God – *Thank you, Jesus.*

It is written in Joshua 1:8, "This Book of the Law shall not depart from your mouth, but you shall meditate in it day and night, that you may observe to do according to all that is written in it. For then you will make your way prosperous, and then you will have good success." God reminded the children of Israel how they could achieve good success and prosperity by reflecting on the Word of God at all times.

God wants us to be successful in all that we do; He has called us out of darkness into His marvellous light:

> But you are a chosen generation, a royal priesthood, a holy nation, His own special people, that you may proclaim the praises of Him who called you out of darkness into His marvelous light; who once *were* not a people but *are* now

the people of God, who had not obtained mercy but now have obtained mercy.
(1 Peter 2:9)

How wonderful it is to know that the Lord has chosen us, that He has made us into His own people, that we may know victory in our lives; as a result, we proclaim His praises.

To know success in Christ, it is important to read and study the Word of the Lord; it is also good to read as much as we can books of encouragement that have been written for our benefit.

If we are going to be good successors of God's kingdom in Jesus Christ, it is also crucial to have a consistent prayer life, for when we spend time with God, it becomes evident in the depth of our relationship with the Lord as well as our relationship with others and overall attitude. The following is noted in Hebrews 13:20-21:

> Now may the God of peace who brought up our Lord Jesus from the dead, that great Shepherd of the sheep, through the blood of the everlasting covenant, make you complete in every good work to do His will, working in you what is well pleasing in His sight, through Jesus Christ, to whom be glory forever and ever. Amen.

Therefore spending time in His Word and in prayer gives us the fuel and the ability to live a life that is pleasing to Him. We become completely equipped to fulfill our God given destinies when we allow God to work in us through His Word and through prayer. Furthermore, God is exalted and sin is conquered in prayer.

As we develop a relationship with the Lord, He will give us a vision for our lives, and this vision will move us forward; this vision will become our driving force.

Even when we fall short or fail, God is merciful and remains faithful to His promise for our lives if we hold on to Him:

> "I *was* so foolish and ignorant;
> I was *like* a beast before You.
> Nevertheless I *am* continually with You;
> You hold *me* by my right hand.
> You will guide me with Your counsel,
> And afterward receive me *to* glory."
> (Psalms 73:22-24)

Even through your trials, don't stay away from the sanctuary of the Lord. This is when you need Him most. When you are weak He will be your strength. We must always keep our focus on the Lord, and not on the situations going on around us in our time of storm. Trust in the Lord and He will bring you through. Pray and exalt the Lord, even when you don't see results right away. Never give up. Continue to press your way through, and you will receive the blessing God has for you. Never back down when you are faced with trials and opposition. To retreat is not an option in order for you to inherit the promises of God. Go through the journey. Jesus never backed down from anything. Don't let discouragement stop you from pressing on in the Lord; even through the wilderness and in the valley, the Lord will give you peace.

I would like to add that complaining never helped anyone. Just look at the children of Israel; they were fed with manna from heaven – with the food of angels – and they still complained and were never satisfied. They did not appreciate what the Lord had done for them. Let us never get to the place where we become ungrateful for all the wonderful things that the Lord has done for us. Let us be happy with the simple things in life, learn to enjoy what we have at this present moment, and consider the less fortunate who have so little yet are often thankful and cherish all they have. Let us remember that we are blessed, and not take for granted all the benefits we have inherited through the suffering of Christ Jesus, for He came that we would have life more abundantly. God is good and the supplier of our needs. Our enemy, the devil, does not want us to take hold of our inheritance; he wants only to steal it and deprive us of it. "The thief does not come except to steal, and to kill, and to destroy. I have come that they may have life, and that they may have it more abundantly" (John 10:10). As we can see from this scripture, the Lord has promised us that we will have a plentiful life in Him, so let us walk continually in His footsteps according to His will, and make a success out of our lives and ministry for God's glory.

We have the victory through our Lord and Saviour Jesus Christ, even though we may sometimes hinder our own blessings. In order for us to access the victory we have in Christ, we must activate it by prayer, for the more time we spend in prayer, the more power we will receive to overcome the flesh, and the more we will be led by His Holy Spirit.

It is good for us to give God thanks and the praise He deserves. It is also good to be at a place where we are willing to sacrifice our time and effort for the Lord, being fully dedicated in all that we do for Him.

As Christians we should desire to be just like Jesus. He is at the center of our lives and people should see us and know that there is something different about us. Jesus, the Word made flesh (John 1:14), is still alive today and He is always working through His people. And by the power of the Holy

Ghost He has given us the strength, authority and ability to manifest the Word of God and be witnesses to the world that Jesus is the one and only true and living God. It is only through Him that we can be saved: "Nor is there salvation in any other, for there is no other name under heaven given among men by which we must be saved." (Acts 4:12).

We are also to walk in power and authority just as Jesus did, for He said it in His Word that we are to do even *greater* works than He did: "Most assuredly, I say to you, he who believes in Me, the works that I do he will do also; and greater works than these he will do, because I go to My Father" (John 14:12).

We are not powerless; this is why every believer needs the Holy Ghost. It is written, "But you shall receive power when the Holy Spirit has come upon you; and you shall be witnesses to Me in Jerusalem, and in all Judea and Samaria, and to the end of the earth" (Acts 1:8).

It's important to have the Word of God in us so that we may not fail in life for lack of knowledge. The beauty of His Word is that Jesus – the Word of God made flesh – will live in us and He will draw out who we are in Him. Challenge yourself to go deeper into His everlasting Word; each scripture always has another to support it and there is no limit to how deep you can go.

In order to have true success in all you put your hands to for the Lord, let God lead you and then follow in obedience. Then everything will work out for your good. God will show Himself to be God, and crush the plans of your enemy. Step out in faith to fulfil your God given calling, stay focussed, and keep your mind on what God has called you to do, for it is the plan of the devil to send distractions your way to take you off course. Be strong, courageous and patient as you endure what is thrown at you, and you will end up enjoying the fruits of your labour.

I have learned to do what God has placed in my heart and not pay attention to what people around me are saying, because there will always be critics, and it is always better to please God rather than man. Let's put our trust in God; He looks out for our best interest for He knows us better than we know ourselves. We put our own limits on what we can do, but the Bible reminds me that: "I can do all things through Christ who strengthens me" (Philippians 4:13).

There are also times in our lives when we are to just listen and observe, be slow to speak and quick to listen (James 1:19) because this is simply what God needs you to do at that time, and obedience is the key. Too many times we as humans take situations into our own hands only to find that we have made a mess of things and we end up missing the mark. This is why it's important to let go and let God have His perfect way in our lives, as this is what will bring true success. What God has for you and what He places in your hands, ask your spirit to just accept and receive it in Jesus' name, for He knows that if you are faithful with the little He places in your hands, you will be fruitful and faithful in all you do.

It's amazing to see how God has entrusted each and every one of us with His work, to see how confident He is in us. He sees us as the finished product of who He created us to be, not as others see us, nor how we see ourselves.

Remain confident in the Lord and believe that you can do all things through Him. God is looking for faithful and humble servants to move by His power: "Now to Him who is able to do exceedingly abundantly above all that we ask or think, according to the power that works in us" (Ephesians 3:20). We need to tell ourselves that we will remain confident in the Lord, and this confidence comes through a life of prayer and studying the Word of God; it also takes a dedicated relationship with Christ Jesus. He is the only one who knows what is in our hearts. Be willing to step out and take that risk, whatever it may be that you feel called to do, for the Lord will allow you to stand out and shine for His glory.

When someone recognizes the light of the Lord in me, I give all praise to Jehovah because He is my Redeemer whose loving concern for me never changes. "And those who know Your name will put their trust in You; For You, Lord, have not forsaken those who seek You" (Psalms 9:10).

It's important to remain at the place where you are well disciplined in your thoughts and in your ways: "Keep thy heart with all diligence; for out of it are the issues of life" (Proverbs 4:23).

More importantly, look beyond yourself and see the needs of others; step out of your comfort zone and the things *you* want. Capture the greater vision and continue to work by adding to the kingdom of God, for we are all used in different ways and the ultimate goal of all assignments is to win souls into the kingdom of God.

True success comes when you place God at the head of your life. When you make Him your priority, everything else will line up in its rightful place.

I've learned from experience that we should avoid running ahead of God and try to do things our own way, for we may end up in a ditch that God will have to pull us out of. We must wait patiently on the Lord for His timing is best. God's unmerited favour is so awesome because although we may not deserve it, He still reaches out for us no matter the state we are in. And once He touches us, we will never be the same.

The more I think about it and see all the corruption that is taking place in the world today, the more I see God as the only real solution. The devil has deceived so many people and countless lives are in a whirlwind of chaos. I used to think that success was based on all the material things that one could possess, but as I grow in spiritual maturity, I am beginning to better understand why a child of God should never covet what the world has to offer, for all of it is only for a season, while God's blessings are everlasting. God is the captain of our destiny and we must not doubt Him because it is impossible for Him to fail – He has not failed me yet and I can guarantee that He won't fail you either.

Go loves us unconditionally; there is no greater love. As I look back on my life and see how far the Lord has brought my family and me, my lips never refrain from giving Him Praise.

My children have never been in trouble with the law; God Has kept them from violence, drugs and addiction, and I can only boast in the Lord. It is so important for us parents to cover our children under the blood of Jesus on a daily basis. I am not saying that my children are perfect, but I give glory and honor to my God for keeping, healing, directing and providing for my children through this journey of life, and I tell you that I will never stop fasting and praying for them. The Lord has helped me realize that as a single mother, I did what He required of me to do for them and more, and now that they have grown into mature young men, it's time for them to take God at His Word for themselves. I have taught them the Word of God and I will continue to teach, encourage and guide them, for as a parent, this is my God given mandate to bring them up in the admonition of the Lord.

Family devotions have always been an awesome time for us to enjoy together in the presence of the Lord. The Lord has instructed me to let them take turns and lead our family devotion. This entails opening in prayer or choosing who will do so, selecting the scripture, leading the testimony time and giving words of exhortation – basically opening our devotion time the same way it would be done for a service at church.

I truly believe my children are called to be great in the kingdom of God. We are all called to be great in Christ, so let us use our gifts to the glory of God.

At a certain point in our journey, God may call us to stand alone, and it's not that He wants us to be alone; He wants us to be at that place where we are sold out for His purpose to be fulfilled in our lives.

You might feel alone at this present moment but you are not alone for God is with you. People may not understand what is happening with you, but it's ok because it is between you and God.

When you get instructions from the Lord, just be faithful and obedient, and watch God move in your life, bringing change to your situations, to your family and even to your community by His power. My prayer is that God would use us all to bring change to every life we come into contact with; that they would see us and notice the light that shines bright in us, for it is not about us but about Jesus and His love for the entire world. *Oh how I love him.*

The greatest part of my life is the sweet relationship I have with my precious Lord and Savior. God has been so good to me; I have no complaints. He has never failed me and I know that He never will. I have learned from experience that true success comes from having a personal relationship with the Lord. My life was never the same after I gave it to Christ. Everything fell into place when I began to live in the will of God, and the closer I got to Him, the more I began to know His voice, and my faith has only grown from there.

People can replace unhappy memories with new happy feelings, but they still have to deal with the hurt and pain of the past before being able to truly enjoy the future.

I also think it is imperative for parents to take the time and communicate with their child or children to be aware of what's transpiring in their lives. I know from experience that the earlier you start having open communication with your children, the more they will feel that they can share anything with you, right from a young age. I made it a habit of always sitting with my children whenever they came home from school or from an outing, having them share with me the good and bad things that had happened that day. I would specifically ask them to share what they liked or didn't like about their day. This helped in building a good habit of open communication with my children and also created a bond between us.

As a child, you look up to those who are older than you. Your family members are people who normally should take care of you, provide for you and care about your well-being. Although this wasn't the case for me as a child, despite all the ups and downs, God brought me through!

All my pain and suffering just seemed like the norm for my life, but what I went through should in no way be seen as normal. If your childhood was similar to mine, I am here to help you realize that you need to tell someone, no matter how hard it may seem for you, because no one should have to live with this type of burden and fear. All the unhappy childhood memories of abuse that I suffered at the hands of my uncles were very painful, and I thought at that time that these memories should remain a secret. However, now I see that life is meant to be enjoyed with the freedom of being able to share with others.

CONCLUSION

There are always situations in our lives, whether big or small, which cause us to wonder if anyone cares or understands what we're going through. Well, I can tell you firsthand that Jesus knows and He cares. Jesus loves you, regardless of how you or anyone else feels about you. We are friends of the Lord, and He wants us to share all of our deepest, and even our darkest secrets with Him.

What secrets are you keeping? When you hold on to these secrets, you are depriving yourself from enjoying the abundant life the Lord has for you, and from every opportunity that are to come your way.

Secrets have a way to bring shame, and as a result they keep you from getting involved in the things you enjoy best. Living in the darkness of your troubled past is not acceptable to God, and that is for your own good. The Lord wants to deliver you from everything that would be a hindrance in your life. God has a purpose for every one of us. I encourage you to seek the face of the Lord in prayer, and to find out what His perfect will for your life is.

Confess to God the truth of what is troubling your mind so that He can free you from it. The Lord wants to set you free from your past; please don't wait any longer. Surrender all to the Lord. There is healing and deliverance for you even right now; just believe it and receive it. The Lord is waiting with arms open wide.

The Word of God says, "If we confess our sins, He is faithful and just to forgive us our sins, and to cleanse us from all unrighteousness" (1 John 1:9). God has offered us forgiveness, and the best thing we can do for ourselves is to confess our sins and accept His forgiveness. The hardest part is usually forgiving ourselves.

What may have happened to you was not your fault, and God is the only one who can take away the guilt and shame. Again, just surrender all to the Lord and He will see you through.

The Lord wants us to share our deepest hopes, thoughts and desires with Him, even though He is El-Shaddai, the Almighty God and Creator of the universe. This shows just how much the Lord wants us to communicate with Him. David the psalmist wrote, "I love the Lord, because He has heard my voice and my supplications" (Psalms 116:1). God does hear your cry; He will come to your rescue and He will be on time.

Don't let yourself be tormented by your past, and most importantly, don't seek revenge. Let the Lord fight your battles. Jesus never fails.

There is nothing too hard for the Lord, and there is no wound that has been dug so deep that the Lord cannot heal. God is a healer, He's a miracle working God, and He loves you more than you can imagine.

The fact that He died for us shows us just how loving He is. We only need to open our hearts to Him, and He will heal us and bless us with only good things.

> For I know the thought that I think toward you, saith the Lord, thoughts of peace, and not of evil, to give you an expected end. Then shall ye call upon me, and ye shall go and pray unto me, and I will hearken unto you. And ye shall seek me, and find me, when ye shall search for me with all your heart.
> (Jeremiah 29:11-13 KJV)

What a wonderful promise...

You Will Soon Recover

Focus on the goals you have
And don't lose sight
Believe God's plan
For He will keep you walking right

Take a look at yourself
With God's point of view
And you'll find a blessing
That's just for you

The devil may have tried
Many times to take your prize
And all he ever leaves you with
Are lies upon lies

But with the Lord's strength
And all the needs that He'll supply
You'll soon realize
That your victory is nigh

So when battles in your life
Appear at every door
And every time you turn around
The devil seems to roar

Remember all the devil has of yours
 You'll soon get back
Satan can't transcend your strength
He won't succeed in his attack

That day is coming soon
When your battles will be won
You'll notice every step you take
Will make the devil run

So keep your eyes on Jesus
And listen for His call
For you will soon recover
Yes - without fail, RECOVER ALL!

Poem used with the permission of Cryssy Savage Hall

About The Author

Evelyn Walters was born in Kingston, Jamaica and raised in the beautiful country of Canada. She is the proud mother of two amazing sons (whom she loves to the moon and back) and the grandmother of three precious grandbaby girls: Aaliyah, Myha and Kyrah.

Her relationship with her Lord and Savior is most precious to her and what has kept her through life until now. Her passions are for pastoral care, foreign missions, Christian counselling, and serving people in need – namely women, children and the elderly.

Evelyn delights in taking walks in the park and beholding the beauty of God's creation. She also enjoys traveling, reading, writing, playing the piano, cooking for people, and spending quality time with family and friends. Evelyn has learned to enjoy the simple things in life.

Evelyn's message is one of hope, healing, forgiveness and restoration. She hopes to encourage those who have been through traumas of their own to get to a place where their wounded souls can rejoice again.

Made in the USA
Monee, IL
01 February 2020